Pen of Gold

PEN OF GOLD

*and Other Poems
and
Essays to Inspire*

Nora Mae's *Daughter*
ALICE HEIN SCHIEL B.S., M.ED.

XULON PRESS

Xulon Press
2301 Lucien Way #415
Maitland, FL 32751
407.339.4217
www.xulonpress.com

© 2022 by ALICE HEIN SCHIEL, B.S., M.ED.

All rights reserved solely by the author. The author guarantees all contents are original and do not infringe upon the legal rights of any other person or work. No part of this book may be reproduced in any form without the permission of the author.

Due to the changing nature of the Internet, if there are any web addresses, links, or URLs included in this manuscript, these may have been altered and may no longer be accessible. The views and opinions shared in this book belong solely to the author and do not necessarily reflect those of the publisher. The publisher therefore disclaims responsibility for the views or opinions expressed within the work.

Unless otherwise indicated, Scripture quotations taken from the King James Version (KJV)–*public domain.*

Scripture quotations taken from The Message (MSG). Copyright © 1993, 1994, 1995, 1996, 2000, 2001, 2002. Used by permission of NavPress Publishing Group. Used by permission. All rights reserved.

Scripture quotations taken from the New King James Version (NKJV). Copyright © 1982 by Thomas Nelson, Inc. Used by permission. All rights reserved.

Paperback ISBN-13: 978-1-66285-914-4
Hard Cover ISBN-13: 978-1-66286-262-5
Ebook ISBN-13: 978-1-66285-921-2

Dedication

This book is dedicated to my sister Virginia Ann Asselin who died on August 13, 2021 and my sister LaVerne Chollett who died on June 11, 2022. Both were monumental inspirations in my life.

Table of Contents

Dedication v
Introduction ix

Pen of Gold! 1
Commercial in the Making. 2
Life is SO SWEET. 6
I am a Hunter's Wife 14
Weight Watching 20
Padre Island National Seashore 25
Best Day of My Life 26
A Pledge of the Heart 34
Angels in Disguise. 38
Raising Kids 42
Pinnacle of Life 54
Amazing Things! 56
Unexpected Catch. 63
I Recommend Jesus 69
Alice - "in Wonderland" 71
Expectations 80
High Praise 86
"Friendly" Law Enforcement. .87
Hidden Treasure 96

Introduction

Welcome to my third book Pen of Gold! It is a collection of essays with some poetry sprinkled throughout. The writings range from light accounts of experiencing life in the country to a few heavier pieces which emphasize truths worthy of being preserved in print. My poem "Pen of Gold" declares the power of the pen "binding hearts! binding souls! awakening bright minds!" My writings repeat and help spread the fruit that we all need – love, joy, peace, longsuffering, gentleness, goodness, meekness, temperance, and faith. I pray that you will reflect these more clearly to those around you as a result of immersing yourself in these writings.

Thanks to my husband Bill for helping me get this book completed. He has been my number one encouragement with all my events promoting my first two books: <u>Nora Mae, a Remarkable, Insignificant Person</u> (biography) and <u>Old Yellowed Hat</u> (devotional) and was my main support in finishing this project. Bill and my sister Sarah Muñoz, a bilingual language expert, did all the proofreading of my manuscript.

Also, thanks to my sister Sarah for allowing me to include her poetry masterpiece "I Recommend Jesus" in this book.

I want you to enjoy the stories. I hope that the thought-provoking pieces will connect with you and will also help preserve golden truths for generations to come. Get started reading and enjoy!

Note: the abbreviation "Lol" has somehow found its way into my essays. It is a cell phone texting gem and means "Laugh out loud."

Note: my books <u>Nora Mae, a Remarkable, Insignificant Person</u> and <u>Old Yellowed Hat</u> can be ordered from xulonpress.com, barnesandnoble.com, and amazon.com. <u>Nora Mae, a Remarkable, Insignificant Person</u> was a winner of the *John Weaver Excellent Reads Award* for Non-fiction: Biography.

Pen of Gold!

O' Pen! Simple instrument possessing might!
The punch of your recordings brings minds new light.
A pen captures details and ideas of men
Emblazoning them on porous minds drawn in.

The worth of pen and paper cannot be told.
Writings' value must be close to that of gold!

Proverbs 25:11 says:
Words fitly spoken are like apples of gold.
In pictures of silver they're strikingly bold!

"Gold" brings me thoughts of heat, refining, and fire.
Words withstanding opinions: favor and ire.

The written words are mentioned in scripture too.
God directs the pen; the words settle like dew.

In Jeremiah chapter thirty, verse two
God said, "Write all the words I have spoken to you."

My words can fly to a place I do not see.
If I write them down, copy them enough,
they will fly 'til eternity
arrives and sets us all free
from limitations of our humanity.

Pen of gold! Words to hold! Engraved line by line.
Pen of Gold! Pen so bold! Your message is enshrined.
Binding hearts! Binding souls! Awakening bright minds!

ALICE HEIN SCHIEL B.S., M.ED.

Commercial in the Making

In the early 1960's my little sister Sarah and I were in elementary school. Not that that really influences this story, but just to let you know that I may have been in third grade and she in first. We had vivid imaginations and loved to play all sorts of things. One of our favorite things to play was "restaurant." We each had our own restaurant and would be owner, cook, waitress all tied up in one character. We each had certain menu items that were exclusive for our restaurant.

Once we both caught the chickenpox at the same time. We were broken out from head to toe with these little blister-like bumps and could not go to school. The blisters would ooze and drain if you scratched them, and we were warned that scars would be the result. So we tried very hard to not scratch even though the bumps did itch, especially when they started to dry up. We did a great job entertaining ourselves to keep our minds off the itching and I guess we were successful because neither of us got scars. The initial fever that accompanied the onset of chickenpox did not last long and so it seemed to us that we just got to stay home from school and play. We played "restaurant" to our hearts' content. My specialty sandwich was a Mustacromia sandwich! It was a slice of white bread with mustard spread on it, and then folded together. I had two versions of the sandwich that I offered. One was simply mustard on white bread and the other one was mustard on white bread with dill pickle slices in the middle. I loved this one! It was really tart to the taste buds and could wake you up in a second. We used actual bread, mustard, and dill pickles. One of us offered another sandwich that was Miracle Whip (a salad dressing) spread on bread and then folded and a few others. But nothing could compare to my Mustacromia delight! It was superb! We played our restaurant game every day that we were home with the chickenpox (and many other days)! What fun we had!

Fast forward twenty-three years! At this time I was the mother of three children. They too loved to make sandwiches for snacks. One liked "energy" sandwiches which were made with peanut butter, banana, and honey mashed together and put on bread. The three-year-old loved Miracle Whip sandwiches which were simply Miracle Whip spread on wheat bread and folded together.

At this time our small town was growing. Some new grocery stores opened up. The new stores, of course, had special sales and I would still shop at our hometown store (Klein's Supermarket), but would also try some of the sale items from the new stores. I compared the prices in the sales papers which were delivered to our mailbox and planned my grocery shopping according to price. The new stores had their own brand of salad dressing, comparable to Miracle Whip, but in a different looking jar. My kids did not like the cheaper salad dressing for their ham sandwiches or for any sandwich, for that matter. They refused to eat it. But the price was so good and I didn't think the taste was that different. Of course, I am mostly a mustard eating girl when it comes to sandwiches, hamburgers, hot dogs, etc.! Maybe I was being fooled.

One day I got a brilliant idea, "I will wash out one of the Miracle Whip jars. I will buy the cheaper salad dressing and transfer it to the Miracle Whip jar while the kiddos are sleeping. They will unknowingly eat it and all will be well!" So that is what I did.

The three-year-old came into the kitchen in the early afternoon wanting a snack. "I want a Miracle Whip sandwich."

"Okay," I said. I went to the refrigerator and got out the Miracle Whip jar which held the discount salad dressing sandwich spread. I put the bread and the jar on the table. We worked together to fix his snack sandwich the way he liked it. I smiled.

My three-year-old took one bite. He laid down the sandwich and looked at me with wide eyes. "Sometimes I like Miracle Whip sandwiches. Sometimes I don't!" He jumped down from the chair and ran off to play.

Busted! Over the years I often thought about this incident and thought what a cute commercial it would have made. This three-year-old was able to taste the difference in the salad dressing sandwich spread! And what a cute expression, "Sometimes I like Miracle Whip sandwiches. Sometimes I don't!"

Needless to say, I had to give up on the cheaper product. My family preferred the real thing! Miracle Whip it had to be.

Life is SO SWEET

I think that there is healing in singing, particularly if it comes from your heart. We live in the country, a tiny slice of wonderful! Actually there are people all around, but the wooded area gives you the feel of being in your own space. Behind our property is located a small plot of land not developed. Otherwise there are people around; you just can't see them because of the trees.

One morning I was doing a routine duty, taking scraps out to the compost. The compost is in an area away from the yard, but still a mowed area. It is located about twenty feet from the garden. When I go to dump scraps I am always very careful to watch for snakes. Four years ago my husband was bitten by a copperhead in the garden. Over the period of seventeen years that we have lived here I have killed two or three of those myself. One time I almost stepped on one when I made the short trek to the compost! I saw the snake as I was about to place my foot, so in mid-air I jumped over it. I am always careful (well, almost always). This year I had seen no copperheads.

It was in June. I was carrying my little compost bucket in one hand and two stacked containers in the other. I watched every step I took. The path was clear, no snakes! I dumped the scraps and headed back. I had only gone about twenty feet on my mowed trail when I felt something like a sting on my right foot. "That's stupid! I just stepped on a wasp," I thought. My thoughts quickly readjusted, "It couldn't have been a wasp; you're wearing sandals; you would have crushed it if you stepped on it." I took another step and wheeled around to see this "wasp." Two steps behind me was a large, coiled copperhead, his head still striking the air! I let out a few screams! Bitten by a copperhead! I never expected this! I was careful – on the way out, but not watching enough on the way back. I guess I thought the coast was clear and let down my guard. Whatever! I was bitten.

My husband was in the garden. I yelled to him, "Bill! I was bitten by a copperhead," as I took a few more steps forward. I watched the snake as it slithered across the path and under the yaupon bushes. Sure seemed like it was taking Bill forever to get here. My ankle was beginning to hurt a bit. Bill showed up carrying a tool of some sort. He was walking slowly. Directly, he said, "Why are you limping?"

I repeated, "It bit me!"

He looked shocked, "What? I thought you said you SAW a snake, I didn't know it bit you! Where did it go?"

"It was up there on the trail, about near that hanging limb. Yeah, there. It slithered under those yaupon."

Bill searched, even going into the brush. I headed to the house. I changed my clothes. I knew we needed to head to the ER or at least the doctor; I called my doctor's office and they said, "Head to the ER." I was wearing my new leggings. The ankle was beginning to swell and I could envision them cutting the brightly colored leggings off me. Can't ruin my new leggings! I changed quickly. The pain was gradually getting worse.

"I didn't find it," Bill said as he came in. He was sweaty from head to toe, but then, he always is sweaty in the garden in the summertime. "I need a quick shower."

He jumped in the shower and I began to pace through the house. I started praying loudly. I walked from room to room, my mind totally focused on God.

"Come on. Let's go!" We were at the Emergency Room within about 45 minutes from the time I had been bitten. It was getting difficult to walk. When I would take a step it felt like a million needles poking. Sitting, I was okay. The guy checking us in asked, "How long ago did you say? Close to an hour? Get in here." He took my name and led us to the back.

The pain was going up now. I was thinking, "I am either praying LOUDLY in here or I am singing!" I opted for singing. This was on Wednesday, June 19th. The prior week, June 10 – 14, I had been singing Vacation Bible School Songs for two hours in the afternoon with the three energetic girls helping me lead and then, of course, every night at church. Two weeks before that I had been learning the ten new songs and the dances that went with them. Those VBS songs were in my head and came bubbling out, "Every good thing! Every good thing! Every good thing, every good thing! ...... You're the reason for anything that lasts, every second chance, every laugh. Life is SO SWEET!" Hmmm – doesn't quite match the situation. So I tried the verse: "There will be days that give me more than I can take, but I know that You always make, beauty for my heartache. Don't wanna' forget or take for granted that it's a beautiful life we live. I'm not gonna' miss the moments like this..." That's more accurate. But, I started thinking, "I wonder what is good about this." I kept on singing, "Every good thing, every good thing!"

The nurse came in, smiling at my singing, and drew a circle with a marker around the bite. The pain was becoming unbearable and lying on this hard bed, I discovered that if I put my right leg straight up in the air, the pain was less. So I did. I couldn't do the Vacation Bible School dance routines on the small narrow bed I was lying on so I got the idea to do them, high in the air, with my feet! At least that way, my hips were even, sort of. I kept singing the song until I felt like I was wearing it out. The nurse and the practitioner came in and out. I wanted to change songs, but was having difficulty thinking of the start of another one. Yes! I finally did. "Wherever You lead me, I'm gonna' follow. I'm trusting You,

God; You are good! Life will be crazy! Wild and amazing! I'm trusting, You, God; You are good!" Oh, yeah, the verse: "I want to live each day like anything can happen. Can't hardly wait to see what's next. I want to face this world with wonder and excitement! Face every challenge, every day! Wherever You lead me, I'm gonna' follow...."

I kept singing. The practitioner came in, "Is she delusional?" she asked Bill. He was sitting in the chair, texting our kids. "Well, she usually is sort of, just like this," he commented.

They put in a port for morphine, but I didn't want morphine. The singing was working just fine. Each hour the nurse drew a larger circle as the swelling increased in my ankle and lower leg. They gave me a tetanus shot. It had been a really long time since I had had one. "Keep it elevated," they instructed and put a stack of thin hard blankets under my ankle. The bite was on the ankle, on top of the foot. The position was so awkward! My back was starting to hurt. So my legs went up in the air again, and I was singing! I had been here for about three hours now and was getting hungry. I usually have breakfast and then a snack around 10 AM. I had a few peanut M&Ms in my purse for an emergency hunger situation so I asked if I could eat them. "Yes!" Sweet. But there were only like ten in the already opened package and I was still hungry. I asked Bill to get me some chips. My son came by and prayed for me. One of my Pastors came by and prayed also. A girl came with a computer and checked me in. The practitioner came again. She said, "My girls have been going to VBS this week. They are singing these songs too."

Wow! The pain seemed manageable. I needed to go to the restroom so they brought me a wheelchair. I sat up. When I tried to step to the chair, I simply could not do it! The pain was horrible! That needle feeling! My strong arms did most of that trip to the bathroom and, then, I was glad to be lying on the narrow bed again. The nurse came in and hooked up an IV so I would not get dehydrated. They were watching for any allergic reaction to the bite. One's throat can get swollen and cut off breathing. There are a number of serious allergic reactions that can occur. I kept on singing. Several workers stopped in to see me – the singing, snake-bitten girl (maybe, old lady, naw, couldn't be).

After about a total of four hours, I just collapsed. My singing stopped. I tried to prop my leg. That stack of thin blankets put me in such an awkward position and they were so hard. When the nurse came through again I asked if she could reposition them. "Sure!" She brought me a pillow, and then a few more pillows. I almost fell asleep.

A girl with a computer came in to register me. "We already did this," I said.

"Oh, Okay." She smiled and wheeled the computer out.

After about five hours a new nurse came in, "I am going to take you out. Just as soon as we get this IV stuff out, you can go." She helped get the tape, etc off my arm.

My original nurse came rushing in, "I am taking her out."

"No, I will do it," the other nurse insisted.

"I'm doing it!" the nurse who had been with me, in and out, all day said emphatically.

Wow! Here they were fighting over me, fighting over who would get to take me out to the car! Well, maybe, walking outside was the least hard duty on the schedule or something, but it made me feel fussed over!

Bill went to get the car. My original nurse was the one who took me out. She talked as we went. My pain was still real, but it was evident that I wasn't going to die from it. I was new to Medicare and was wondering if Medicare allows old people to get bitten by snakes, or if I was gonna' have a bunch to pay. Whatever! (I guess my secondary insurance kicked in too. It was covered.)

"Every Good Thing! Every Good Thing!" Maybe the good thing was that I got a tetanus shot. It had been a while, could have been, about thirty years since I had had one.

"There will be days that give me more than I can take, but I know that You always make beauty from my heartache" I was singing again. My church provided crutches for me to use when I first got home. I had a cane (a pretty one with pink roses on it), but the crutches seemed like they would be more efficient. I was mostly sitting around with my leg up because that stupid "needles" feeling attacked every time I tried to walk. I was doing fairly well with the crutches, I thought. I seemed to have the rhythm down. I went toward the kitchen and, for some reason, I turned back to face Bill. When I turned, I lost my balance. Between the stiff crutch and the "needle feeling," I couldn't correct. Splat!! I hit the tile floor flat on my back. I rolled over, then crawled, crying.

"If you are getting off balance, let go of the crutches!" Bill offered.

I did not answer. No more crutches for me! I went back to the trusty cane.

It took me about ten days to get over the bite. The first days were the worst. I had thought it would start getting better as soon as I got home from the ER, but that was not true. It finally seemed like I had reached the peak after three days. The swelling started to subside and the pain became less and less. My friends told me about a teacher bitten by a copperhead who had to be off work for six weeks. I felt really blessed. It had been only ten days and I was feeling better. And I was singing, every day.

Bill said to me, "It didn't take you as long to get over the bite as it did me. Maybe the snake didn't get you as good."

I'm like, "You are kidding me, right? I probably screamed more than you did! The snake didn't roll over like I thought one might if it bit me (LOL), but it sure got me!"

Bill continued, "No! I only meant that the swelling in my leg seemed to go almost all the way to the knee. Yours didn't seem to go more than halfway up the leg."

"Give me a break!" Here we were comparing and arguing about snake bites. Not many couples can enter that conversation. "Well, to be honest," I said, "If you had tried singing yours probably would have been healed more quickly too!"

Dancing with my feet in the air

I am a Hunter's Wife

I am married to a hunter. Not a surprise. I knew he was a hunter before I married him and I did it anyway. He was a country boy; I was a small town girl. He grew up in a family of hunters. His dad and his three siblings all hunted. My personal experience with hunting was limited to eating really good sausage from my brother-in-law's success. My husband Bill has always tried to include me in the fun.

When we first started dating, I was attending Bible college. Midwest Bible Institute had strict rules about dating in those days. All boys had to ask the Superintendent Earl Pruitt for permission to take a girl on a date. I was really glad that Bill was the one to ask for permission. Brother Earl seemed like a strict Father God figure to me. He was one of those men who carries God's presence and you could see it in his eyes. He was an able Bible teacher and a friendly, nice man, but I felt like his eyes knew what I was going to say before I said it. Bill was totally okay with the asking. Besides asking Brother Earl for permission to go on a date, all dates had to be double dates so guys had to plan well. That being said, our first date had to be postponed because Bill got a west Texas hunting trip opportunity.

The date was rescheduled. This first date was a trip to watch Tomball in the high school football playoffs. The year was 1971 and the game was at Kyle Field in College Station, Texas. Instead of a double date, it was a family affair. I liked his family. His mom went. His older brother, his older brother's wife and their two kiddos completed our entourage.

The MBI double dating was actually lots of fun. We first dated in December so spring semester found us in some unique double dating situations. I met Bill at church and the first five months (of our eighteen months of dating) we saw each other most often at church. It was a twenty minute drive from school to church and I didn't own a vehicle so I always needed a ride. There was a young married couple attending MBI and I sometimes rode with them to church. After church they would invite Bill to go with us to the Dairy Queen. They would always tease about "being on a date." So here we were double dating with a married couple. A few times Bill picked me up from work (JC Penny's at Northwest Mall, Houston) right before a school holiday. He brought his young niece and nephew along so we wouldn't violate the school rule. My second year at MBI we had regular dating partners. Jackie Crabtree and Freida Booth from Arkansas were number one on the list.

It was a rare occasion when we took our first walk in the woods on a Sunday afternoon, just the two of us! It was either a holiday week-end or we were between semesters. The woods were beautiful, Bill's playground. Suddenly he ran ahead, around a bend in the trail and when I got there he was nowhere to be seen. For a moment I was nervous. I had no idea which way to go except stay on the main trail. It was a bit frightening. I just kept walking. Then I heard a whistle; I heard it again and again. As I passed under a large tree he jumped down. It totally surprised me and took my breath away! He was laughing. He was just what I needed – a sense of humor! I'm not sure why I was so lacking in the sense of humor area, I must have not been paying attention when it was handed out! He had climbed up in one of the trees and was delighted to have scared me. We laughed a lot! He loved the woods.

After we married, the first extra thing we purchased was a chest freezer, for the meat from the hunt! We got that even before we got a television. We've never been without one. He mostly processes his own meat and there is always some hunting season going on.

For a period of about fifteen years Bill took a break from hunting. It was when our children were small; he started becoming involved with their activities. He coached soccer, t-ball, baseball, football, basketball, and track for a few years. The next few years found us ball gaming with the children at school every fall. After our three oldest graduated high school, his inner hunter came alive again. This time he switched to bow hunting.

I've been on a lot of hunting trips. I've helped track the animals, sometimes through brush, sometimes through cactus. I've stayed in some pretty meager hunting cabins and in some great ones. The most bare bones place we stayed we lovingly called "the Ritz." The outside walls were single boards with cracks between. But it did have a wood heater which Bill hooked up. Before long, believe it or not, it was cozy. (Bill is a wood heat expert!) We had our own hunting camper for a while. One year Bill wanted me to accompany him on a hunting trip, but there was no indoor plumbing at the place. He went early in the summer to prepare things for the hunt and he installed plumbing, yes, an indoor bathroom! When we arrived on our hunt that fall, there was water running out of the outside wall of the cabin! Whoever hunted just before us forgot to turn the water off when they closed up. Weather temperatures dropping below 32 degrees had caused the pipe to break, and when the sun came out...you get the picture! Without complaining at all, Bill turned the water off, headed to the nearest town to buy supplies, and had the repair done before night. Yes, he's always gone out of his way to make the "roughing it" less rough. Once, at a different lease, there was a snake in the commode when we arrived! He calmly took care of the snake.

I've sat for hours in a watch tower blind (a gun hunter's blind), 12 feet high in the air, 200 yards from the action with my young son and snacks and drinks and card games to entertain us, if need be, as we watched eagerly. The animals usually provided a great show: birds, rabbits, squirrels, turkey, fox, hogs, deer, and axis deer. I've sat in ground blinds with animals 3 feet away never detecting my presence. (Was a bit scary when it was huge tusked hogs at dusk!) I've sat in a tree blind, next to the hunter, ten feet up, leaning against a tree on a little 2 feet by 3 feet platform observing the deer feeder 15 to 20 yards away.

I've ridden up "mountains" in open jeeps with supplies piled high, bouncing wildly, and holding on with white knuckles. I have autographs from a couple of TV Outdoor Channel hunting show stars. One even gave me an autographed coin bag for my coin purse collection! I've also been the camera girl, capturing the action to thrill the viewer. Never made any award winners, but figured out how to use the simple camera. I am a pro at doing still shots of Bill and his prize!

My hunting adventures are priceless! Nowadays, where we hunt, it is more like a home away from home. We are blessed. We even have TV, so no missing football games! Well, since the football boycott we have been watching hunting shows on the Outdoor Channel. It is still a retreat from our normal routines, but there is little roughing it.

Yes, I am married to a hunter. We have LOTS of hunting videos. Bargains at Academy have caused us to accidentally have two of certain videos. When you have so many, it's hard to remember what all you do have. But, no biggie, it was a sale!

My husband has two sets of clothes. One set gets laundered with our regular detergent and is put away in his chest of drawers or in his closet. The camouflage set of clothes is laundered using special scent-free laundry detergent and is stored in a large green bag with certain small 2-inch discs which smell like dirt. Of course, these little discs are really called "earth scent wafers" and help the hunter smell like the outdoors. We have scent-free shampoo, body wash, deodorant, field spray, dryer sheets, and even expensive scent-free body suits. But, no worries, we bought it all on sale! The scent-free stuff is needed by bow hunters because they have to be much closer to the animals than the gun hunters do. It is only used in connection with the hunt.

Bill almost always includes me on the hunting trips; however, I have not developed into a hunter. Bow hunting is pretty much the standard and I can't pull enough poundage to kill an animal. Yes, Bill taught me to shoot a bow and I have a few camo duds. We joined a local bow shooting group. Each week we went to the range a few miles from where we live and entered competitions, hitting lots of different targets. I practiced at home, too, and was pretty accurate. I still own my bow, but haven't used it in a while now. Our local range relocated farther away and we have plenty of targets of our own, so the weekly treks ended. Most recently, the grandkids have used my bow to practice their skill. I haven't even tried to shoot it in a few years. I really do need to get my bow out; I am married to a hunter!

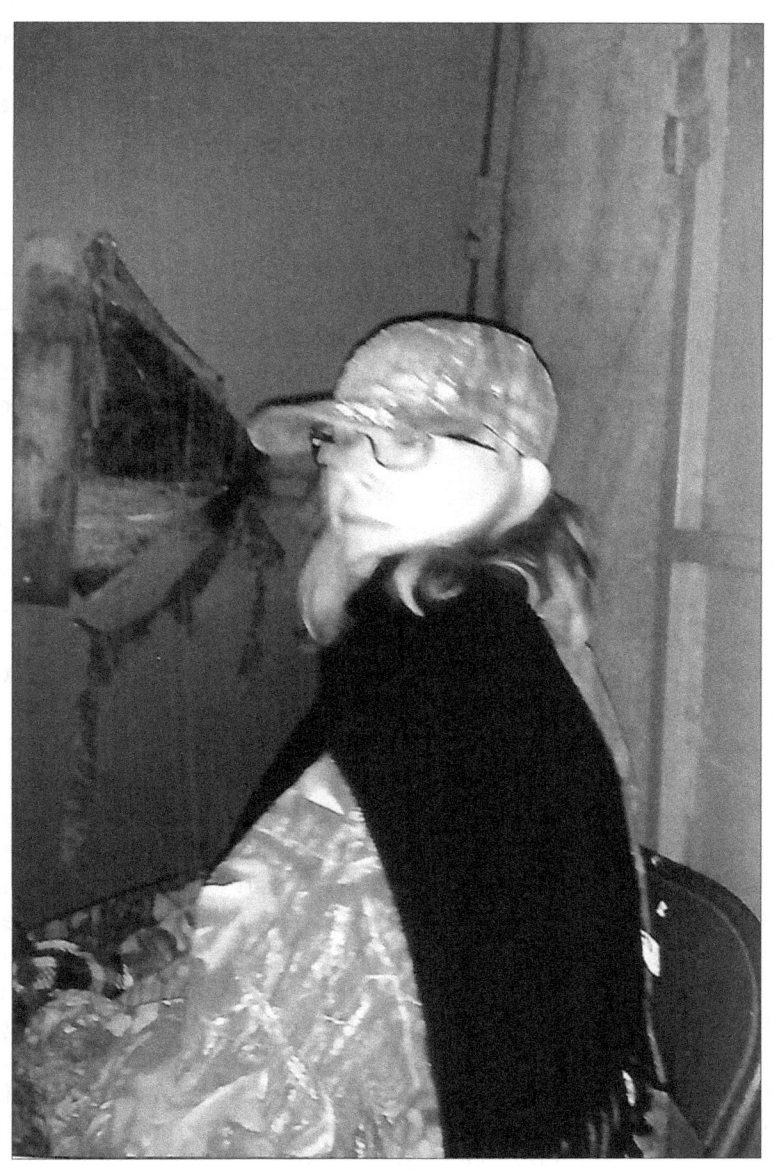

Weight Watching

Weight watching has always been one of my specialties. At Bible college Sister Pruitt reminded us to watch our eating. She said that most students are not used to eating three well-planned meals each day, so they gain weight. I didn't think that I could lose a bunch of weight so decided to take her advice and watch it.

My first conscious decision about what I ate was to limit calories. I bought a little book on counting calories and started tracking my numbers. I decided to cut out breads and desserts. I was fairly strict on myself and it worked, I did not gain any weight during my two years at Midwest Bible Institute. I even lost a few pounds.

I got married the summer after graduation. The little calorie counting book had become my guide. I had some cooking experience, not a lot. I had learned to cook in Homemaking class at Somerville High School where Mrs. Lois Broach was the instructor. My mom encouraged my cooking and bought ingredients for the three or four meals I could do. We included them in the family meal planning almost every week. I could make a tasty tuna casserole and a great Frito pie! I had learned to do homemade biscuits, but didn't practice that recipe as much. At Bible college I ate in the cafeteria all the time, so no cooking skills were needed. The Dean of Women Susan Fry (now Susan Pruitt) gave me a Betty Crocker <u>Cookbook for Two</u> as a wedding present. That book was a life saver and greatly expanded my cooking expertise. Instructions included things like how many hours ahead to thaw your roast, how much time to allow for peeling potatoes, etc. Bill thought I was a fairly good cook because dinner was always ready when he got home around 5:30. He didn't know I had started early in the morning, planning, thawing, tracking each little thing, putting together meals as the cookbook suggested. I knew about the four food groups and checked the meals against that knowledge. He probably would have thought that I was silly to put so much effort into cooking exactly to the letter, but he enjoyed the result.

When I became pregnant with my first child, I read the little bit of material the doctor gave me. A friend told me that she had gained seventy pounds with her first pregnancy which caused some physical issues near delivery time. She later lost the weight, but I wasn't so sure that I would have the discipline to lose a lot of weight if I gained it. I again determined that it would be better for me to not gain so much in the first place. I purchased a scale and began weighing every morning. (Did I mention that I am a bit too serious?) I recorded the numbers just like the doctor suggested. After the baby was born, my weight was down. The baby's first year it was all I could do to keep from becoming a "bone." There was so much to do for the baby! It went from nursing to warming bottles exactly right to warming food in a plastic bowl that was made with a double side. You put hot water between the two liners and it took a bit of time to warm it by natural convection; then it took time to spoon feed the baby. Sometimes I would realize in the afternoon that I had not yet fed myself! I was always cooking a well-planned meal in the afternoon so Bill would not be neglected too badly.

After my second child was born, I had to do a better job of overall meal planning because now I had a toddler eating as well. We had time management training at church and I learned to make a simple, weekly, three-meal-a-day menu. I based the menu on meals from my Betty Crocker cookbook. By using a menu, I saved time at the grocery store because I made my grocery list based on the menu. I saved time each day because I simply looked at my plan and thawed whatever was on it. I didn't have to think about what to cook. After I did the first menu, the next one took me less time to do. I learned to love always having a menu.

I faithfully recorded my weight with each pregnancy and I never gained too too much with the babies. Years later though (me in my thirties) I found myself needing to lose ten pounds.

The birth of a preemie grandchild caused me to walk a lot from the parking garage to Texas Children's Hospital in downtown Houston. I lost five pounds without trying. Getting the next five pounds off took a lot of doing. I went back to my "weighing everyday" strategy and began recording my numbers again. If I gained a pound, I immediately watched my intake the next day. I know that professional trainers recommend that you only weigh one day each week and just keep up with that because you normally fluctuate from day to day. I find that I prefer weighing each day because in a week there's no telling how much I could gain! (Did I mention that I'm a bit serious?)

Today I am in emergency mode. I gained a pound two weeks ago and it's still hanging around. My weight goes down for a day and then it pops back up again. My regular eating rhythms haven't phased that pound one bit! So I am taking measures of self-discipline. I am in my sixties now. I am going to make myself write down everything I eat the next few days. That usually helps me find where my problem is: am I eating too much of something or am I drinking too much V-8 Energy juice? Or, seriously now, am I eating too many dark chocolate kisses (I am allowed a few!) or am I drinking too much Dr. Pepper? Oh, the real culprit pops up. I am brutally honest here. If that doesn't do it, then I'll crack down on "what time am I eating supper?" If need be, I'll track it and make sure I do not eat after 5:00 PM. You can see, I am hilarious, but I am serious! Get in line, girl. I don't want to age prematurely because of too much weight. Aging has enough challenges without adding overweight to the issue! Some things I can't do anything about, weight is not one of those. At least, so far in life, it has worked that way.

Two days later – Well, well! That extra pound went away. Writing down what I ate was enough to make me curb my intake. Yippee! I'll let you know if it's still gone in a week (sneaky pound).

One week later – I did it!! The extra pound is still gone!

Two months later – no comment.

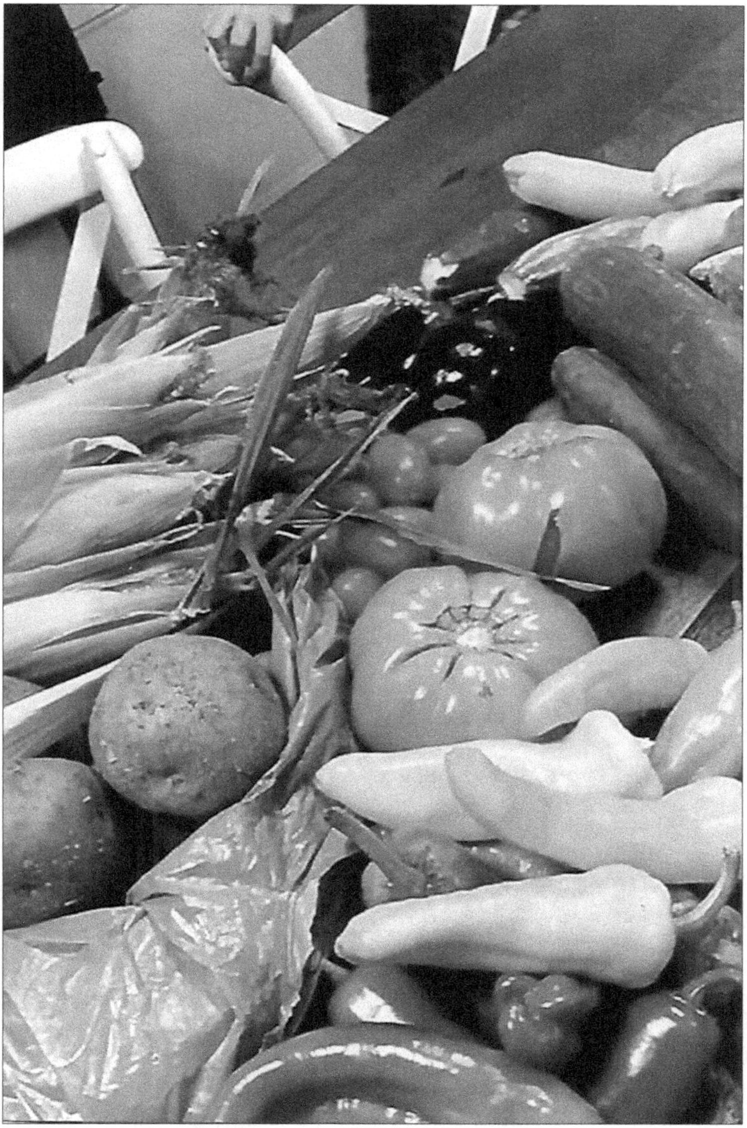

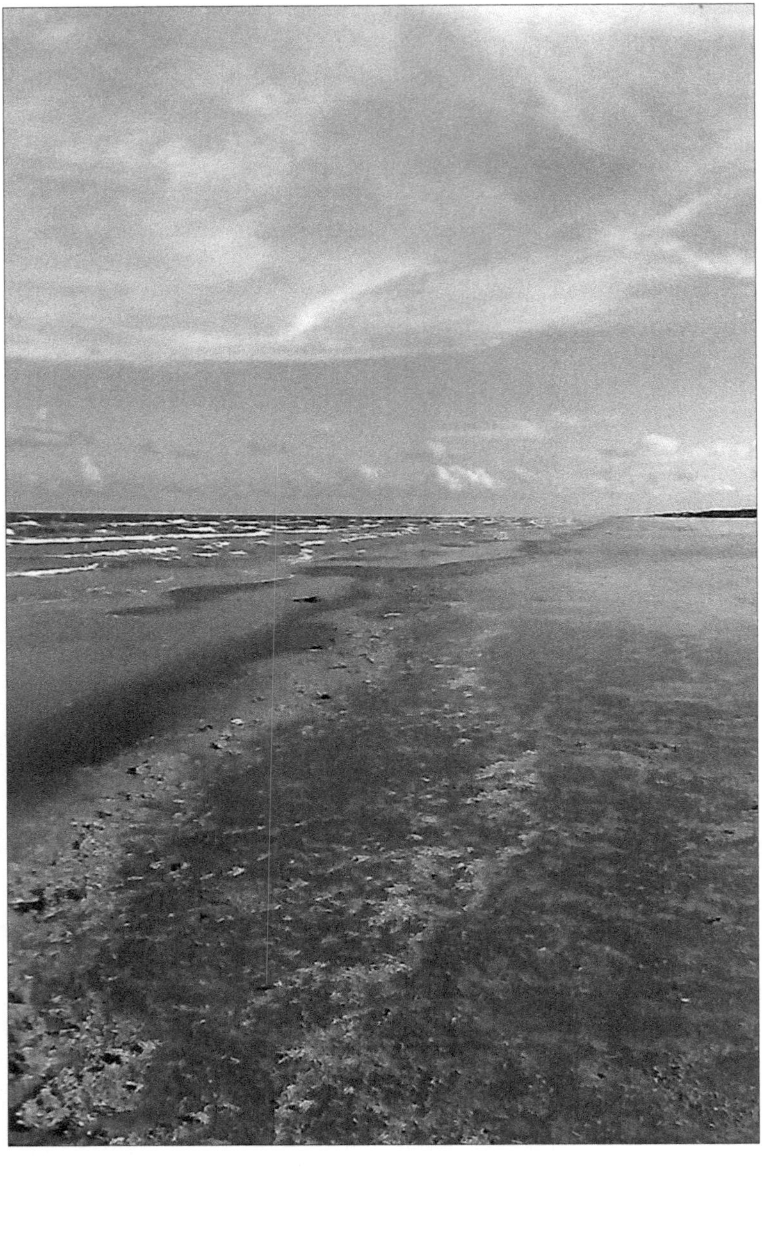

Padre Island National Seashore

As crowds disappear, we keep going.
The half hour drive turns almost desolate.
After a while an eerie feeling
Surrounds me; I consciously dismiss it.

"Visitor Center" signals left turn
We climb wooden stairs to a sprawling deck.
At last! Water in sight! Daylight burns.
We rush down the boardwalk, nature beckons.

The sand crabs scurry into their holes.
The birds are running in the water's lace.
It seems we own the beach as we stroll
And sense the power that made this loud place.

The Gulf of Mexico roars loudly
As it kisses the shore that wants to nap.
The wind is refreshing, yet tricky.
It tries again and again to steal our caps!

We perch on top a picnic table.
Don't want tiny crabs to bother our feet.
As time stands still the scene is stable.
We drink in a picture our hearts will keep.

Best Day of My Life

Growing up I often heard friends comment, "I can't wait until I'm older!" In high school one of my friends was frequently saying, "I can't wait until I'm 18. I'm outta' here!" When I returned home from Midwest Bible Institute for a visit, this friend and I met at the "drug store" (local pharmacy that also had a soda fountain and hamburger shop). We talked and laughed like old times.

"I can't wait until I'm twenty-one," she giggled!

Here it was again, a longing for the future. Something clicked in my brain: "the future can't be all my focus; I have to enjoy the now. I need to remember to see each day's blessing." So I decided to live as if "every day is the best day of my life." I made it my motto.

I try to look for what the day offers – new experiences, new people. "What is God showing me today?" Almost fifty years later I am still seeing each day as a special gift. A few people have commented to me, "But you've never experienced tragedy. You've never had bad things happen. You don't know real challenges."

Boy, are they misinformed! They do not really know me. We all face challenges, loss, heartache, disappointment, rejection. But we also have triumphs, victories, accomplishments, happiness, and acceptance. Being from a large family (I have ten siblings) I may have experienced more instances of hurt and faced more of life's challenges than most. My sister Sarah Muñoz has a great perspective on this, writing, "God's comfort is extended to His children in proportion to their hurt; the greater the pain, the greater the comfort." When I am crushed or in despair it becomes my best day because I learn something new about God. I feel Him closer to me.

The year 2020 will be remembered as the year of pandemic – COVID 19. I want to tell my Covid story. Our Thanksgiving 2020 was a much smaller celebration than usual. We had a total of ten people at our home. For the past twenty years my sister Lourene Falk has hosted a family Thanksgiving in Bellville, Texas. She rents the American Legion Hall and more than 50 of us ascend on the place full of anticipation and conversation! Everyone brings their favorite holiday foods and desserts resulting in a huge, delicious feast shared by all. But 2020 was the year of the pandemic so the family celebration was cancelled. For the first time in many years we celebrated at home with a small group of ten. My daughter and her family left early that evening.

On Friday morning my son and his family headed home. My daughter brought her girls over for piano lessons. Just as the second lesson ended she got a call from her husband. She hung up the phone while saying to us, "He tested positive for Covid!" I said, "Oh my! Is he okay? What are his symptoms?" And then, "we've all been exposed!" We all felt okay. Being the optimistic person that I am I ran to get my thermometer to prove that I was unaffected. I was disheartened to see that it read 99.1. But I felt okay. I said nothing, but my mind was racing, "How long is the incubation period? Maybe I am infected. I wonder what to expect. What will happen next? I am not part of the elderly community, but I am 67 years old; and older people are affected more! Geepers." My daughter headed home.

I got out my Bible and started looking up healing scriptures. I wrote Psalms 91:9,10, 11 on a card and taped it on the inside of my kitchen door.

"Because thou hast made the LORD thy refuge, even the most high thy habitation, there shall no evil befall thee, neither shall any plague come nigh thy dwelling. For He shall give His angels charge over thee, to keep thee in all thy ways." (King James Version)

My mind was racing, "What do I need to do?" I grabbed my cleaning gloves and my Lysol disinfecting wipes and began sanitizing all the doorknobs, all the commodes, the TV remotes, and all the furniture in the living room and dining room. Just in case something was left on the furniture Bill brought in my antique "low-riding" rocking chair from the guest bedroom for me to use the next two days. I thought I'd read that the virus can live on nonliving objects for two days. I would avoid my recliner. Of course, no one had sat in Bill's recliner but him, so I wiped it down and he continued to use it. I removed the tablecloth and headed to the washer. There was a load of clothes in the dryer. Hmmmm. I said to Bill, "I can wash the clothes, but you will have to fold them so I don't infect you. I have fever, you do not." He folded the load of clothes. After the second load he said, "You know what? We are not quarantining from each other. If we go down we'll go down together." I responded, "Yes, dear."

Bill had no symptoms but we decided to quarantine ourselves for fourteen days. We have friends with health issues so we wanted to be cautious. He called the ones who usually stop by our house and told them to stay away for fourteen days.

I grabbed my None of These Diseases book by S.I. McMillan, MD (11th printing, 1971) and started reading some more scriptures. I wrote other healing scriptures like Isaiah 53:5 "...and with His stripes we are healed" (KJV) on cards and put them on my mirror, on my kitchen counter, and all around the house to remind myself that God is with me.

I started thinking, "What is going to happen to me?" I kept reading the scriptures and nothing unusual seemed to be happening. I felt tired so I sat in the rocker a while. Then I went to bed. My fever that night was 100.1 – not much.

On Saturday morning the fever was gone and it never returned. I was tired the next two days so I rested. On Sunday we kept our quarantine and did online church.

Tuesday is our regular grocery shopping day so Monday night I explored and conquered my first online grocery shopping spree. Delivery? No, they do not deliver in our area, but we could do "contactless grocery pickup." The order would be ready at 8:00 AM Tuesday. Bill went alone. He parked in the labeled area at the end of the store. A text arrived, "the groceries are ready" and he responded, "I am here." Someone sporting a Covid mask came out with the loaded cart and signaled a window roll down. Bill obliged. "What is your name?" Name confirmed Bill popped the trunk. The employee put the groceries in, closed the trunk, and waved a "good-bye." Bill was excited when he arrived home, "I can't believe how easy that was! No wasted time!"

I was feeling well so I did my normal chores. I was never sick so I never went to the doctor. I stayed home and did not go out at all. I communicated with my daughter daily. Three in her family (including her) tested positive, but had few and only mild symptoms. Medical advice she received was, "If all four of you are COVID positive the 14 day quarantine is good. If one of you is not infected the family quarantine is 24 days." What?? So they had their other daughter tested even though she had zero symptoms and she also tested positive! My daughter told me that one of the predominant symptoms is loss of taste and smell. It was hilarious! Every day I went around sniffing things – lotions, fruit, flowers, perfume. Nothing had a scent. I always concluded with something that I thought I could smell.

I cleaned house. It was hard to keep Bill who never had any symptoms inside. He decided to go hog hunting. "Hey! I am quarantining from people, not from animals." He didn't get anything on his hunts but he went several times.

The second Monday of the quarantine I said, "It's time to get our grocery shopping done." Bill said, "I like that online shopping. It is really simple. I drove up there, they loaded it in, and that was it!" I retorted, "That's because you didn't do the order. It took me hours to do it. It is your turn to put the order together." So Bill made the order, well, we sort of did it together. He spent a while at the computer, but still thought it was much less time consuming than walking through a store. I happen to like walking through a store!

We kept our fourteen day quarantine and I was beginning to think that maybe I had not had COVID. But in the weeks following I started noticing that my sense of smell was returning. The lotions, fruit, flowers, perfume, etc. that I had been sniffing during the quarantine suddenly had scents, very vivid scents! I really had lost my sense of smell and now it was back!

What about my taste? During the quarantine I noticed that green beans tasted like cardboard. I didn't relate it to COVID because I thought that "no taste" meant zero taste impulses, not different taste impulses! I tried to fix the green beans. I added butter, garlic, pepper, onion powder, and even bacon to them. They still tasted cardboardish. On the grocery order I ordered different brands of green beans and different types of green beans. I even purchased Green Giant brand kitchen sliced green beans which had been my favorite for years – before their price got so high. I was surprised when those tasted yucky too. I couldn't figure it out. The green bean Issue was the only taste issue that I really noticed. A month after our quarantine green beans started tasting great again!

I feel sure that I did have Covid. My symptoms were very mild, but then, my daughter and her whole family had mild symptoms. I don't doubt that it is a serious disease and I had a friend who died from complications related to Covid. I also have friends whose three year old fell into the swimming pool and was retrieved, but later was breathing "funny." As a precaution they took her to the ER. When leaving the facility they were told that her paperwork would list Covid as the cause. What?? It would show COVID because it involved breathing issues! Wow! My friends told the doctor that he had better not document it as COVID.

To me 2020 is the year of healing! Millions around the world were healed of COVID 19.

The best day of my life is each and every day! During my Covid quarantine I learned to be kinder to myself. I learned to think more about my health. I learned to take all 4 tablets in my "women's pack" daily. I have always been a busy person with my days jam packed. I would open the daily vitamin pack, take two of the four tablets which took quite an effort to swallow, eat a bite, and then jump into my day. My morning routine included getting dressed, making the bed, reading my Bible, praying, watering some of my flowers and I seldom got back to the other two tablets until the following day or two days later....or three days later. During the quarantine I learned to slow down and take all four tablets, plus I added extra tablets of vitamin C, vitamin D, vitamin B-12, and zinc! And I continue to take all of that every day! This "little girl" who has taken very little medicine her entire life has to take those vitamins and tablets one at a time, with water. It takes a little time, but my water consumption is also up. That is another plus.

Yes. "Every day is the best day of my life" continues to be my life's motto. When I was in my thirties I discovered the writing of a famous author who stated it much better than I. Ralph Waldo Emerson penned,

"Write it on your heart that every day is the best day in the year. He is rich who owns the day, and no one owns the day who allows it to be invaded with fret and anxiety. Finish every day and be done with it. You have done what you could. Some blunders and absurdities, no doubt crept in. Forget them as soon as you can, tomorrow is a new day; begin it well and serenely, with too high a spirit to be cumbered with your old nonsense. This new day is too dear, with its hopes and invitations, to waste a moment on yesterdays." Well said, Mr. Emerson.

Embrace today. It is the best day of your life!

"Every Day is the Best Day of My Life"

A Pledge of the Heart

The wedding ring is an important part of our culture. It is the universally recognizable symbol of marriage. The wedding dress will yellow, the flowers will fade, but the wedding ring is metal, made to last forever. In some families wedding rings become priceless heirlooms. The tradition of wearing rings has evolved. In earlier tradition the guy and gal both wore engagement rings and then the bride received those two rings at the wedding. (This brings all sorts of sizing issues to my mind, but maybe early rings were easily adjustable. I know I could never have worn Bill's ring. We did exchange high school rings, but he had to wear mine on a chain around his neck. I wore his on a lapel pin which was fashionable at the time.)

My parents married in 1932, a year related to the Great Depression in the United States. During those Depression years wedding rings became simple bands. All things of great value were appropriated to the war effort (World War I). I don't remember my mother Nora Mae ever having a wedding ring. In the United States the tradition of men also wearing wedding bands started during World War II. Soldiers wore the bands as comforting reminders of who was waiting for them at home.

When Bill and I got married it was common practice to have a double ring wedding ceremony. We were both excited to wear our rings – each declaring to the world – "I am married!" We wore our rings faithfully but took them off to shower or at night.

I took mine off to do certain chores like washing dishes. After I had my first baby it seemed I left it off more frequently around the house. The stone could inadvertently scratch that little bundle of motion, plus I didn't want to get the ring all yucky with diaper changes, etc.

Bill took his off at night, but he always wore it to work. He once had a scare on the job when the ring got caught between metal and he struggled to get his finger loose. Shortly after that we heard about a guy whose ring got caught as he was working and they had to cut his finger off. That did it! Bill quit wearing his wedding ring to work. It was not a big deal. It was safety. Before long he wasn't remembering to ever put it on.

In the early 1980's the larger diamond came out of my ring set so I did not wear mine. The diamond and the rings remained in the ring box on top of my dresser. My sister-in-law and her three littles came to visit one day. Our six kiddos were playing and one of the littlest got my ring box. When I saw the child with the box I retrieved it at once. The rings were there, but my diamond was missing! My heart sank. How I searched that day and the next week. I was afraid to vacuum the carpet. I prayed that I would find it. One sunny morning I was at the kitchen sink. I turned around and a sparkle just under the sofa in the living room caught my eye. I ran. It was my diamond! I put the ring box and its treasures in my top drawer. Little hands could no longer access it freely.

When I returned to college in 1986 I started wearing a game machine ring with a single fake stone. It was not a genuine wedding ring, but still that universal symbol. I wanted it to be known that I was taken, no extra drama needed. It must have worked, I never had to fight off the guys! I wore that game machine ring with its single large gem for probably 15 years. My daughter-in-law started working at a jewelry store and Bill got her to help him get my diamond reset as a surprise for me. I was so excited and thrilled to be able to wear my real rings again.

Bill's ring remained in the ring box in the top of his chest of drawers. We really never even thought about it. We were busy raising kids and tackling life. After we retired, I found the ring when I was cleaning one day. "You know, there is really no reason for him not to wear this ring – I mean, not wear it every day, but to church or when we go out." But there was a reason: the ring did not fit Bill anymore!

I took the ring and Bill to the local jewelry store and we had them resize it. He said, "I don't really need a ring to remember that I am married."

"But you need a ring so other people will know you are married! Don't blame me. It is not my fault that you are married. You are the one that asked me to marry you, I did not ask you."

He started wearing the ring again, reluctantly. "It doesn't feel right. It bothers my finger. I don't even remember to put it on." Slowly he got in the habit of wearing the wedding ring again.

But then one day when he went to put it on the ring box was empty! We searched carefully around his recliner, under his recliner, inside the recliner, but did not find it. We looked in his truck, on his chest of drawers, everywhere, but didn't find it. I prayed we would find it. We did not. I did not want him to lose the habit of wearing the ring again. "We will just have to get another one!" I said. No resistance!

To the jewelry store we went. I bought him a new band. It was not precious metal, but it fit perfectly and looked great!

About a year later we replaced Bill's recliner. When we took the old chair out I cleaned the spot thoroughly. I saw no ring but combed my fingers through the carpet. I started the vacuum cleaner. I ran my fingers through one more time. I felt something! I almost missed it, but there was his original wedding ring, the one I had given him in our wedding ceremony, the ring that symbolized our youthful hopes and dreams, the one that symbolized our pledge to each other, the one that made our statement to the world! That priceless piece of metal, the unending circle of promise, was buried in the carpet. How could we have missed it?

And so Bill now has two wedding rings. When we go out he generally chooses to wear the second one because it fits the best.

Recently a friend of ours commented that he and his wife were celebrating their fiftieth wedding anniversary. He stated that he had never removed his wedding ring. Bill and I looked at each other. Our mouths dropped. Then we grinned. At least we had remembered to put ours on before going out this day.

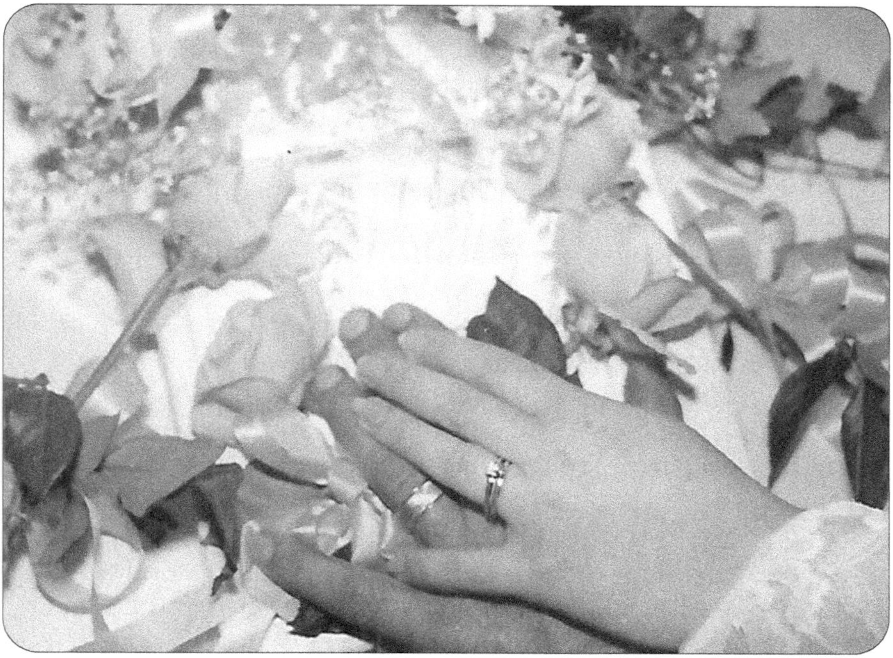

Angels in Disguise

I had turned 68 years old that summer, but when they asked me to lead the music for Vacation Bible School I was not about to tell them that I had not jumped in a while. It had been, maybe, like a year since I had jumped! But I felt sure that I could do it if I just practiced. VBS songs are all about the joyful dancing as much as the words that you sing. In reality they had asked me to lead the VBS music the year before – that was 2020. Sound familiar? It was the year of Covid 19. Vacation Bible School was cancelled because of Covid so I never had to fully learn the songs. The next summer everyone was so excited that we actually could have VBS! Things sometimes change over time, though, and I wasn't sure that I would be asked to lead the music this time. But I was.

It was time to get my dance moves going! I loved helping in VBS that summer. But, I mean, when you are my age it takes a little longer to get everything done. Besides, when you are leading the music you have to practice the songs a lot more. No learning the words and dance moves in one or two go-rounds like the old days! I practiced and practiced and practiced and got the motions down. And, yes, my jump came back. The two girls that I asked to help me lead were both 14 years old. I was not as smooth as the two of them, but I was on it!

The littles (my youngest grandkids ages 7, 4, 3) spent the night with us on Wednesday of VBS week. On Thursday PawPaw picked up the three older girls (ages 14, 12, 12) around 2:00 PM. The eight of us had my home cooked dinner at 4:30. Home cooked, that translates as lots of dishes! We ate, got the littles ready to go, and rushed off to be at the church by 5:30 PM. We were starting at 6:00 but leaders have to be there early, you know. All the grands were picked up right after VBS ended. I gathered my stuff and Bill and I headed home. No biggie, I expected to find my table full of dirty dishes, extra beds still unmade from the morning, few toys and puzzle pieces scattered around everywhere. (Hey – we had a fun day!) Instead I walked in to find the kitchen totally clean! But I only noticed the table first. Wow!

I said to PawPaw, "Did you clean off the table?" PawPaw and the littles had left the church before me and the older three girls. The car seats were in his vehicle.

He responded, "Me, uh, no."

Then I noticed fresh flowers on the table! Hey! I walked a little farther and saw the living room, all clean, everything in place! The bedrooms were cleaned with beds made! The bathroom had been tidied! Wow! I was sure the angels had been here! My son and his wife had cleaned the whole place while we were at the church. What a great surprise!

My mind immediately went back to a similar blessing forty years earlier. Bill was Vice-President of the Alumni Association at Midwest Bible Institute. I was the Secretary-Treasurer. There was a big event coming up at the college and I was in charge of decorating the tables. We also were the owners of Schiel Nursery, a retail plant sale and landscaping business. We were donating the use of plants as centerpieces for all the tables. That meant that I was getting all the plants' leaves polished and putting decorative foil covers on the pots. We had to load all of them for transport. We needed to go early to get everything set up for the event. I had a small baby that I was nursing so she had to go with me. When it was time to leave, my house was not tidied, my dishes were undone. Honestly, the place was a mess!

The baby's cloth diapers were washed, but I had no chance to get them hung out. (You do know what a clothesline is, right? (Hint: It is outdoors.) It is a string or wire about thirty feet long extended about six feet above the ground between two poles. One uses clothespins to attach the washed clothes to the clothesline. The sun and the wind dry them fairly quickly and when dry they smell really fresh. I got my first electric clothes dryer when my daughter was three months old.) At this time, however, I was hanging my washed clothes on the clothesline at Bill's Grandmother's house which was two football fields away. Not convenient, especially if you were pressed for time. So to solve my problem, I did what any creative mother would do; I hung the wet diapers over all the window curtain rods in the house! There were curtain rods in the living room, dining room/kitchen, master bedroom, and in the baby's room. Every curtain rod was used. The diapers were hanging everywhere and would be dry in a few hours. I planned to get them all folded and put away the next day. The house was a mess, but the plants were gorgeous. We left in a rush. There was still so much to do.

Everything at Midwest Bible Institute went according to plan. I got the decorations done, enjoyed the event, and we stayed late to help get things cleaned up. The baby did great! Being so young, she mostly slept. When we finally arrived home, I was dragging. It had been a long exhilarating day and I knew the sink full of dishes awaited as a downer.

We opened the door, turned on the light, and walked in to find the house - clean! All the dishes were washed! The diapers had been taken down and folded! I stared in disbelief. Who could have done this? Did an angel happen by? The answer was even more amazing! A sixteen year old boy from our church Youth Group named Dennis Wallen had done it. How did he even know how to fold a diaper! God is good and He sends blessings to us in ways we can't even imagine.

I am so grateful for these two unexpected outpourings of God's love that I received. Doesn't the Bible say that God pours out blessings upon His children? I'm so thrilled to be one of His! God even blesses the ones who do not choose to follow him. "He sends rain on the just and the unjust."

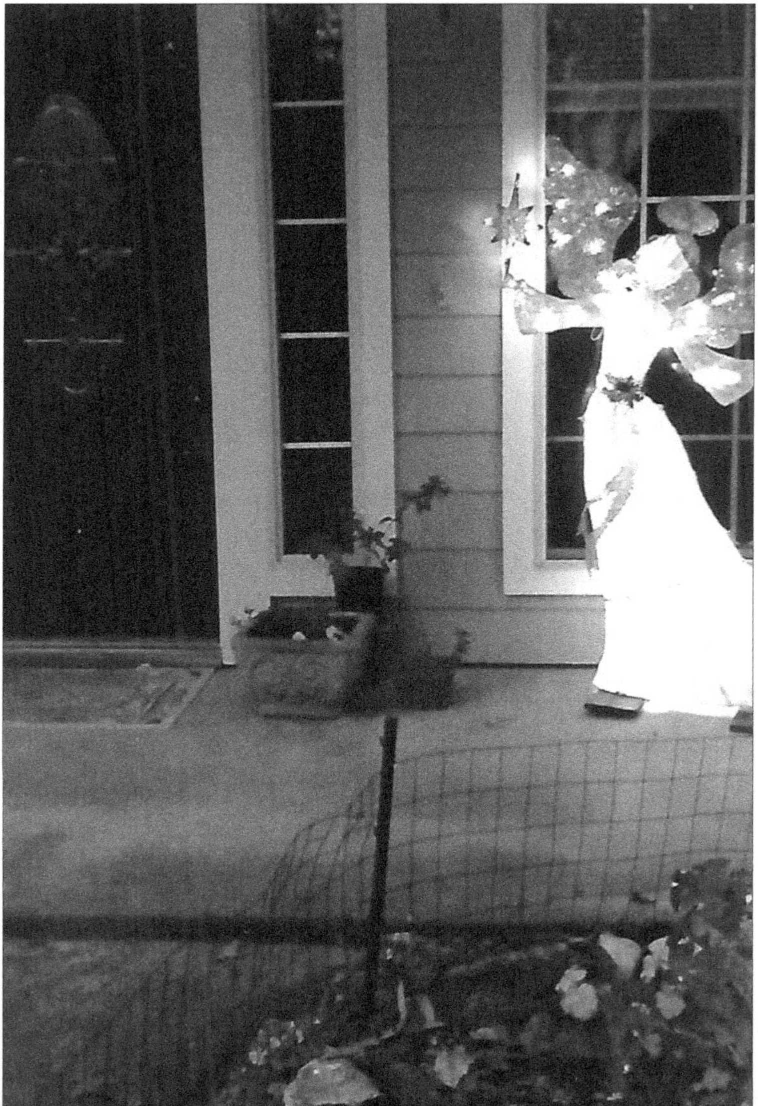

Raising Kids

Preacher Joe. That's what he is known as now-a-days. When we met him thirty something years ago we called him Brother Joe. Joe Williams has been a minister to youth for decades. Most of that time he has been ministering to kids (young adults) living in the streets in the city of Houston, Texas. But years ago he worked with the youth at Living Stones Church where we attended. He asked me, "When are you going to write a book on how to raise kids?" At that time I had not written any books and simply laughed at him. He persisted, "Listen, I am serious. You need to write a book on how to raise kids. Your kids are so enjoyable to be around. They are so responsible and they have a motivation to please God. People need to know how you train them."

I was taken back. I mean, the only preachers you hear talking about how to raise perfect kids are preachers who have no kids! But over the years Joe again and again told me to write a book on raising kids. I told him, "But I don't know how to raise kids. I just know how to pray."

He responded, "There is something you are doing." So I blame Brother Joe for this piece. His words about writing have haunted me again and again. I have tried to think about the most important things in raising kids. I am blessed to have great kids and am thankful for that, but it is nothing to brag about. It is humbling to even attempt writing about it. Recently a young mother came to me asking for advice in training her son. So I wrote down tips to help her and in doing that Brother Joe's admonition came to mind. I wish I had the wit to make this a humorous work, but you are not that lucky! Here goes, Brother Joe, it's not a book, but it is a start.

When I was born my mom was 37 years old and my dad was 47. I'm no dummy. Being kid number ten, I had plenty of examples to observe. If someone got in trouble for something, I didn't do that something. I was more serious than most kids. While other kids were thinking of how it would be fun to push the limit, sneak off, or break the rules, I was analyzing and thinking of all the reasons it would be risky, dangerous, or poor judgment to do so. Plus, I did not want to be a bad example for my little sister. I was almost like an old person trapped in a young body! Lol. I wanted to do the right things. It was totally frustrating to adventurous beings, but it kept me out of a lot of jams.

I heard the Bible concept of sowing and reaping. Galatians 6:7 (KJV) "Be not deceived; God is not mocked: for whatsoever a man soweth, that shall he also reap." I reasoned that by obeying my parents I could be sowing good seed so that I would reap a good harvest – my children would someday obey me! "Yes, I will honor my parents as I want my children to honor me."

As an adult I reasoned, "I do not have a lot of money for my kids to inherit so I will give them God's Word for their inheritance. Proverbs chapter 3 lists many blessings attached to knowing God's Word: 'forget not my law; but let thine heart keep my commandments.' This leads to length of days, long life, peace, favor, health. Imagine being able to give all these to your kids! Verse 15 tells us that the wisdom of God's Word 'is more precious than rubies: and all things thou canst desire are not to be compared unto her.' (KJV) Alright! This is a treasure that I can give my children!"

Proverbs 8:10 repeats it, "Receive my instruction and not silver; and knowledge rather than choice gold." Verse 11 continues: "for wisdom is better than rubies; and all things that may be desired are not to be compared to it." (KJV)

So we went after God's Word. Bill didn't analyze like I did but he saw value in knowing God's Word. We attended God's house Sunday morning, Sunday evening, Wednesday evening, and all special meetings. All memory verses assigned by Sunday School teachers were learned at home. All the Gospel Bill daily confessions for youth sent home by our Children's Pastors were posted on the refrigerator and repeated in the mornings as we got ready for our day. At night I had devotions with the kids before they went to sleep. We read from the children's picture Bible that Aunt Joyce Balke had given them or from the junior Bible that Nanny (Bill's Mom) had given them. Many, many nights the children went to sleep listening to Willie George's childrens puppet tapes. Nicodemus and Barkemaus may have been the ones singing the last song before they went to sleep.

In the summers we always went to Vacation Bible School, Kids Krusade, or church camp – or sometimes all three! Bill and I were puppeteers, teachers, costumed characters, game organizers, music leaders, and even directors over the years. We did bus ministry to bring in other kids. We made it a priority to let our children be filled with God's Word. As the kids grew we also hosted Wednesday night Share Group at our home which included volleyball fun, playing with other kids, <u>Bible</u> study, prayer, and refreshments. Later we hosted youth group cook-outs at our home and volunteered as Youth sponsors at youth meetings.

I never understood parents that did not take their kids or teenagers to church. As Joshua said, "As for me and my house, we will serve the LORD." To Bill and I that meant, "If you live under our roof, you will go to church. We live under the blessing. You will too!"

We branched out to "our kids" community. Bill coached YMCA soccer and tee ball, Little League football and baseball, and youth basketball and track. I ran the scoreboard, kept the official books, was a PTO officer, and was homeroom mother at least once for each of my children. I was a docent for the Houston Symphony Orchestra to my kid's school. We attended all of our kids' games, track events (including

Bill attending out of state), performances, recitals, concerts. Once we had three kids with games at the Little League field starting at the same time; Bill was coaching one team and I was moving between fields! Oh, man! This sounds like a brag, but hey, this stuff is important in raising children. This is the nitty gritty; it is the small stuff that says, "You are the most important thing to me."

Like I said, I don't know how to raise kids, but I do know how to enjoy them. Do not speak negatively about your children! (We had the "terrific two's and three's", not the "terrible two's and three's.") Do not speak negative facts about your child in front of them or where siblings can hear. Your child will receive the message that he/she is not good enough for you if you do this.

Proverbs 18:21a: (KJV) "Death and life are in the power of the tongue…" If your child is disobedient discuss negative behaviors with him or her and state why it is not acceptable. As they become teenagers do not let them be besties with youth who are openly walking in rebellion. You cannot control who they are friends with at school, but you can control whose parties they go to and where they participate in sleepovers. There are advantages in making your home the center of their activities.

Our children are a gift from the LORD. We must train and teach them that they are God's masterpieces. If we do not accept them they cannot accept themselves.

Be consistent in discipline. And don't make punishments too harsh. You have to do what you say you will do.

If you as a parent are wrong, apologize. One of the greatest teachings in scripture is on forgiveness. In The Perfect Blueprint for Happiness, T.E. Murphy says, "Parents are always forgiving while correcting their children." I have had to apologize once or twice over the years. But I walked in confidence knowing that when I corrected my child, God's Spirit would minister to their heart.

As a parent I found these scriptures to be valuable:

> James 1:5 (KJV) "If any of you [parent can fit as a "you"!] lack wisdom, let him ask of God, that giveth to all men liberally, and upbraideth not; and it shall be given him."
>
> Proverbs 23:13, 14 (the Message Bible) "Don't be afraid to correct your young ones, a spanking won't kill them.
>
> "A good spanking, in fact, might save them from something worse than death."
>
> Proverbs 29: 17 (KJV) "Correct thy son, and he shall give thee rest; yea, he shall give delight unto thy soul."
>
> Ephesians 6: 4 (KJV) "And, ye fathers, provoke not your children to wrath: but bring them up in the nurture and admonition of the LORD." The Message Bible says, "take them by the hand and lead them in the way of the Master."

You have to lead your children by your example. How you live your life is important, more important than your words!

Pray this out loud for you and God alone to hear at first. Later your child may hear you pray this:

"Our Father who art in Heaven, You are blessed. You are all knowing.

_____ (insert your child's name in the blanks) is your child, God. According to Galatians chapter 6 _____ has the fruit of the Spirit. _____ walks in God's love. I Corinthians 13 says that love is patient, kind, does not envy, does not boast, is not proud, is not rude, is not self-seeking, is not easily angered, keeps no record of wrong, does not delight in evil but rejoices with the truth. Love always protects, always trusts, always hopes, love always perseveres. Love never fails. I claim this for _____.

_____ is patient

_____ is kind

_____ does not envy

_____ does not boast

_____ is not proud

_____ is not rude

_____ is not self-seeking

_____ is not easily angered

_____ keeps no record of wrong

_____ does not delight in evil

_____ rejoices with the truth

_____ always protects

_____ always trusts

_____ always hopes

_____ always perseveres

(Many times I have also prayed this for myself, inserting my name in the blanks. I have prayed it once every day for a month or more and then again later at different times. Sometimes it may feel like you are just repeating words – BUT those words are actually powerful! Isaiah 55:11 (KJV) reminds us that God's word does not return void! It accomplishes what He intended. It will change your child or it will change you! Lol.)

Father, thank you for growing this fruit in my child.

In Jesus name, Amen

The next list of scriptures are ones to teach your child:

Ephesians 6: 1, 2, 3 (KJV) "Children, obey your parents in the LORD: for this is right.

"Honour thy father and mother; which is the first commandment with promise;

"That it may be well with thee, and thou mayest live long on the earth."

Proverbs 20:11 (KJV) "... for even a child is known by his doings, whether his work be pure, and whether it be right."

Proverbs 25: 28 (KJV) "He that hath no rule over his own spirit is like a city that is broken down, and without walls." Teach your child that when he/she does not control him/her self they are like an ancient city without a wall. Anyone could come in and take their treasure.

Proverbs 16:32 (KJV) "He that is slow to anger is better than the mighty; and he that ruleth his spirit than he that taketh a city."

Teach your child that there are advantages to obeying parents. The Bible indicates that parents are a spiritual covering for their children. If one submits to their parents they will find that to be a valuable attitude. Rebellion is the attitude of Satan.

I Samuel 15:23 (KJV) "Rebellion is as the sin of witchcraft, and stubbornness is as iniquity and idolatry." The prophet was speaking to King Saul and he continued to say, "Because thou hast rejected the word of the LORD, he hath also rejected thee from being king." Saul's rebellion cost him his kingship. Satan was cast out of Heaven because he rebelled against God. He wanted everything his way. We have to dump that rebellious attitude quickly!

"Disobedient to parents" is one of the characteristics of evil humans in the last days. That is found in II Timothy 3:2. We do not want to be identified with evil in any generation. Tell your child, "Wherever you go and whatever you do in life, you will be in submission to some people and in authority over others. You'll be in submission to your pastor, your parents, your teachers, your boss, and even to your husband or wife. Set the pattern right."

People ask me, "Did you spank your children?" Yes, but always in love. To avoid paddling in a moment of anger, I always counted slowly to 10 in my head before the first swat. I always gave only two swats; that was it. When they were small I used a smooth wooden spoon. As they became teenagers I used a leather belt. One spanking seemed to settle the whole house and there might be years before another was needed by someone testing the boundaries I had set. It seemed that after a while someone just had to make sure the boundaries were still there. I never enjoyed it, but by me obeying God's word He was faithful to correct my children's hearts. Bill never had to spank them, but they knew that he would back me up, if necessary.

Proverbs 19:18 (KJV) "Chasten thy son while there is hope, and let not thy soul spare for his crying."

Proverbs 19:19 (KJV) "A man of great wrath shall suffer punishment: for if thou deliver him, yet thou must do it again."

Whether you spank your child, put him in time-out, or take away a privilege – be **consistent**. To me, the spanking is most effective because it settles it immediately. Once the punishment is done, move on. The debt is paid.

One thing I did that brought a lot of peace to my children was to require them to apologize after an argument. I would require them to hug each other and to say, "I'm sorry." They hated this. They did NOT want to have to apologize so they would find ways to work out their disagreements instead of letting them escalate into arguments. Perfect!

Do I believe that you can make a child honor God in their heart? No. But you can teach him/her truth and the Holy Spirit will always remind him/her of it! Proverbs 22:6 (KJV) –

"Train up a child in the way he should go: and when he is old he will not depart from it."

The Holy Spirit works with us doing the work inside our children's hearts and minds.

No, I don't know how to raise kids, but I know how to pray! God is good. He blessed me with wonderful children in spite of any mistakes I may have made. I used His word as my primary tool, but I also read Christian books on parenting. Dr. James Dobson, one of America's leading Christian psychologists, has written many books and articles that are helpful when raising children. Dare to Discipline is one of his best-known works. I found his book Preparing for Adolescence to be a very helpful guide as my kiddos became teenagers. His statement "It's better to prepare than repair…" caught my attention! That book was published in 1978! Even in 2022 his Focus on the Family website continues to make current resources available. You are not alone!

Is your head spinning yet? You cannot do all of this at once, so do not try. Burnout is one thing you do not need! Pray as you begin implementing change in your approach to discipline. Your church is a primary source of parenting helps. Most Sunday Schools teach Ephesians 6:1 and then verses 2 and 3 as memory verses. Sunday School lessons are organized in such a manner that they are recycled every two years as kids move through the <u>Bible</u>. There are different lessons for each age group, but the same truths are taught. Consistently being taught the scripture is invaluable.

Financial stress in a family causes all sorts of compromises. Determine to live within your income. Do not spend more than you make. Learn to budget your income. Be content with what you have. (Plan, dream, and save, but do not spend more than you make. That means credit cards are only for emergencies or for paying the full balance every month. Large purchases like a home or a vehicle should have payments that fit into what you make.) We decided that I would be a stay-at-home mom when our kiddos were small. We intentionally decided to spend less so we could pay for the kids' activities without working longer hours. There are fees for every activity and then, often, there are costumes, accessories (baseball gloves, bats), paints, brushes, team snacks, etc. We lived in a mobile home for quite a few years. We gave up having a new house so we could be free to be a part of our children's activities. We did get a bigger house by adding on to our mobile home, but we did not go into debt to do it. We could say "No" to working overtime because we were not overextended financially. If you are a single Mom and have trouble getting to your children's activities because of work, do not feel belittled. Do the best you can. If you are a dad having trouble getting there because of work, do not feel belittled. Some careers, by definition, require more. Do the best you can. However, if you are choosing to work for bigger and better instead of being with your kiddos, change that thinking and those actions. As a teacher I found that grading papers could sometimes be all time consuming. I learned to grade while waiting for a ball game to start, sitting in line waiting for track practice to be over, waiting for a bus to return, or sitting in the car during guitar lessons or gymnastics practice.

"But godliness with contentment is great gain." I Timothy 6:6 (KJV). My Pastor Kenny Martin II says that contentment is a lifestyle. Be sure you own your possessions. Don't let them own you. Matthew 6: 19, 20, 21 (KJV). "Lay not up for yourselves treasures upon earth, where moth and rust doth corrupt, and where thieves break through and steal: "But lay up for yourselves treasure in heaven, where neither moth nor rust doth corrupt, and where thieves do not break through nor steal: "For where your treasure is, there will your heart be also." Train your children to be content by **example**. It is a peace beyond our understanding.

So, Brother Joe, you can see that I do not know how to raise kids. But I do know how to go after God in such a way that He partnered with me in training mine. I have written the things we did that came to mind. I hope this small essay will help someone with their parenting. "Correct thy son [I say this includes daughter], and he shall give thee rest; yea, he shall give delight unto thy soul." Proverbs 29:17 9 (KJV).

> "Lo, children are an heritage of the LORD: and the fruit of the womb is his reward. "As arrows are in the hand of a mighty man; so are children of the youth. "Happy is the man that hath his quiver full of them…"
> Psalms 127: 3, 4, 5a (KJV)

Brother Joe and me

Pinnacle of Life

The **blessing** of life:
To breathe, to laugh, to smell,
To be a part of God's day,
Of beauty and peace to tell!

The **promise** of life
God's Word outlines for us:
Exhalt and honor wisdom
And she will promote you thus!

The **treasure** of life:
To bring health to your home
"Fear the Lord." "Depart from evil."
It is marrow for your bones!

The **challenge** of life:
Discouraged? Deal with it
Before it overcomes you;
Rise by praying in Spirit.

The **fortress** of life:
The very best people
With you in good and bad times
Give strength – It's just that simple!

The **rewards** of life
Found in keeping God's Word -
Favor, grace, health, long life, peace,
True joy - happy as a bird!

The **sadness** of life:
Separated by death
Soul crushed, breaking heart weeping.
Famine and war stifle your breath.

The **wisdom** of life
Says, "You encourage You."
Don't let depression attach,
Disillusion wants in too.

The **sweet bliss** of life:
Death, a bitter leaven,
Can't conquer a child of God.
Death is our door to Heaven!

The **pinnacle** of life:
Assess each situation.
Then use the rocks hurled at you
To build a firm foundation!

Amazing Things!

Sometimes I do amazing things! Really? Do I want to use the word amazing? Yes, I do!!

I was thinking that my 250-gallon propane tank probably needed to be repainted and I had added spray paint to my grocery list a few days earlier. It had rained a little and the weatherman said that it was supposed to rain more. Hurricane Hanna was intermittently showering us as she turned south eventually making landfall on South Padre Island on the Texas Coast. Therefore, I did not water my plants on this day.

I walked behind the house just to see if any flowers had gotten broken off by the slight winds we'd had. Anyway, I also looked the propane tank over. On the back side of it I noticed that an armadillo had started to dig a hole, right under the tank's legs on one end. It was a fairly large hole, much bigger than the 6 inch ones he normally makes when he locates grub worms, and it angled right under the cement block supporting the large tank's legs. Shocked, I immediately thought, "This has to be filled in. What if the propane tank leans or, even worse, tips over!" I hurriedly got my wheelbarrow and went out to the pasture where Bill was working to ask him where I should get dirt to fill in the armadillo hole I had found. I didn't want compost; I wanted dirt.

He said, "There is some dirt that I still need to level out behind the carport. Take some of that."

Back in May when I was away with my new grandbaby Ezra, Bill had cleared out more yaupon bushes and in July he had built a new larger carport in that area, four times larger than my original one. I pushed the wheelbarrow back to the yard and started shoveling that dirt behind the carport. Now, get this, at the exact spot that I put my shovel in, on the third shovelful, about five inches down I hit something hard! "Oh, a rock!" There was a rock, but what I hit was not a rock; it was a fork. A fork! I shoveled it out, dusted it off, and stood astounded. The fork was from my silverware set that we use every day at mealtime. I had found one of my forks! On our seven acres, the fact that I went to that exact spot to dig dirt to fill the pesky armadillo's hole that I accidentally found, is amazing to me! Wow! My wayward fork is restored!

How did the fork get there? Maybe someone accidentally dropped it when we had friends over for cook-out and Bill's tractor covered it during the carport preparation. Maybe Bill was eating outside when I was out of town and the armadillo stole the fork and buried it. Probably not! There was more than one mound of dirt to be leveled behind the four-vehicle carport, and I had randomly gone to the exact spot to hit the buried fork with my shovel! Amazing! Oh yeah, I already said that. I rescued the fork and Bill and I filled in the armadillo's hole.

I "accidentally" did something special another day! God is good. Bill was out on the tractor clearing a few yaupons. Our new neighbor had put up an eight-foot-tall wooden fence on three sides of his property with a tall decorative iron fence in front. His wooden fence bordered the north side of our property . The deer used to have a trail through that property to ours. The new fence now blocked the deer trail so Bill was clearing a ten-foot-wide path on our side so that the deer could walk all the way down along the fence on this side. He was doing a little more clearing this day.

I was in the house folding clothes when all of a sudden I got the harebrained idea to walk out there and see how much Bill was clearing and to also tell him that I might drive over to my friend Carol's house to buy hand lotion. Carol sells Nuluv Goat Milk Lotion. Funny! All of a sudden I felt like I should go get more hand lotion. As I walked up behind Bill on the tractor, suddenly I heard a noise like metal hitting on metal. It was loud! Did he hit a bucket or something? Bill stopped the tractor and got down.

He then saw me walking up behind him. "Did you hit something?" I asked.

He responded laughing, "I'm always hitting something!" With his hand he signaled toward all the yaupon he had just knocked over. "I hit a few of these!"

"Didn't you hear a loud noise?"

"No. I only stopped to check the property line. I'm almost at the corner." He proceeded to find the corner stake and walked back, unimpressed by my inquisitiveness.

I tried again. "It sounded like you hit a barrel, a bucket, or something." He practically ignored me, so I gave him my message about maybe going to Carol's and turned to leave. There on the ground behind the tractor I saw two fittings of some sort. They were all greasy and were lying on top of the grass! "What are these two greasy things?" I asked.

Bill came around to look. He exclaimed, "My tie rod fell out! I'm not even sure exactly where those came from." He circled the tractor trying to see where the tie rod had come off.

Me, the non-mechanic, but very observant person, noticed a stick about an inch in diameter and fourteen inches long jammed up and sticking out on my side of the tractor. I tried to pull it out. It wouldn't budge. "Could this stick have done it?" I asked.

Bill came around and pulled out the stick that was crammed in. When he did, the rod (power steering rod, technically) fell, hanging. He jumped up on the tractor, started it, and quickly finished to the corner.

I headed back to the house, amazed! I had walked up at just the right moment to find the two greasy pieces of the tie rod. Bill had never even heard the noise when it came off. When he runs the equipment he often puts ear plugs in because of the loud motors, etc. He would have finished, driven over the pieces, headed in, and not have known when or where he lost them. Wow! Timing! Thank you, God! My harebrained idea about the lotion may have been inspired! What a great helper I am.

And that's not all....

Last fall Bill and I did some maintenance work at one of our rental properties. One of my granddaughters and I redid the coating on the deck. The deck was totally cleaned off and we painted the waterproofing sealant on. It dried, looked great, and the outdoor furniture was put in place. A few months later we returned to spray wash and repaint a small utility building near the deck on the same property. Bill and my son-in-law were doing some repair work to the floor of the utility building and also reroofing it. There were at this time a lot of leaves and some small sticks on the deck that we had recoated earlier. The guys needed the drill for a certain task. My son-in-law went and got his power drill, but they could not find the correct sized drill bit that they needed. My son-in-law searched through his set, but one bit was missing. They were discussing how they could accomplish their task and what they should do.

I walked up on the deck, taking a little break from my spray washing project. A few steps in, I stepped on something. It was a small Allen wrench. I picked it up and took another step. I felt something under my tennis shoe again. There among the leaves which wind and rain had blown onto the deck was the very drill bit they were looking for! I'm serious!

That small, tiny metal bit was right there. I had just stepped on it! I don't know how long it had been lying there; it was covered with leaves; but I had just stepped on it! It was not even in the main walking area, it was to the side, but I had stepped on it as they were searching for it! The deck boards have space between them, enough space for such a tiny piece of metal to fall through, but I didn't inadvertently kick it, I stepped on it! It had been lying there waiting for me to find it at just the right moment – the moment that they needed it! That is amazing to me! Yes, amazing!

One more: one of our neighbors needed help getting his garden going. Bill always encourages people with their gardening. He drove the tractor over to Bob's to disc up the garden plot. He had made two rounds of the 30 foot by 50 foot area when the tractor came apart! Something fell off the tractor. It immediately stopped. Bill called me to bring the truck and chain so we could pull the tractor home. While waiting on me to get there he looked through the dirt and found nothing. All eight gallons of transmission fluid had leaked out of the tractor. When I arrived, Bill hooked up the chain, put the tractor in neutral, and I drove the standard truck. We headed home, Bill on the tractor, and me carefully shifting the gears in the truck trying to keep us moving smoothly, without jerking, particularly at the stop sign. Stress City!

The next morning Bob called, "Hey! I was doing a few rounds with my tiller, trying to get the garden started. I hit metal. It must be the part from your tractor. I have it here if you want to come get it."

Bill went and got the piece, but he knew that there was a doughnut-shaped circular piece about five inches in diameter that was still missing. He looked online to see exactly what it looked like. Our friend Tricky (actually J.R., but Tricky to us) came over. He and Bill were talking about the missing tractor piece. "What you need is a metal detector," Tricky laughingly said.

Ding! Ding! "That is a good idea!" Bill answered, "I had one that I got at a garage sale years ago. But I never used it and I have no idea where it could be."

I remembered! I answered, "I know where it is!" I went to the attic, straight to the metal detector! We put batteries in it, jumped in the truck and headed to Bob's. The metal detector worked! In less than two minutes we had the heavy circular piece in our hands. We had had the metal detector for years and this was the first time we had ever tried it. Handy little me! I had remembered exactly where the metal detector was! Bill got the tractor back together without incident.

Bill's grandmother, Grandma Dulaney, taught me to pray when I am in a dilemma or at my "wits end." She taught me that God is very near to us. She needed God's help many times when there was no one else around and God always helped her. In the instances I have recounted for you, I had never even prayed. God helped me when I didn't even know I was going to need help! He is amazing! Grandma also taught me Galatians 6:3 (KJV) "For if a man think himself to be something, when he is nothing, he deceiveth himself." So make sure you get this correction. It is GOD that does the amazing things! He blesses us above all that we can ask or think. Ephesians 3:20, 21 (KJV) says so. "Now unto him that is able to do exceeding abundantly above all that we ask or think, according to the power that worketh in us, Unto him be glory in the church by Christ Jesus throughout all ages, world without end. Amen."

Thank you, Heavenly Father! You are amazing!

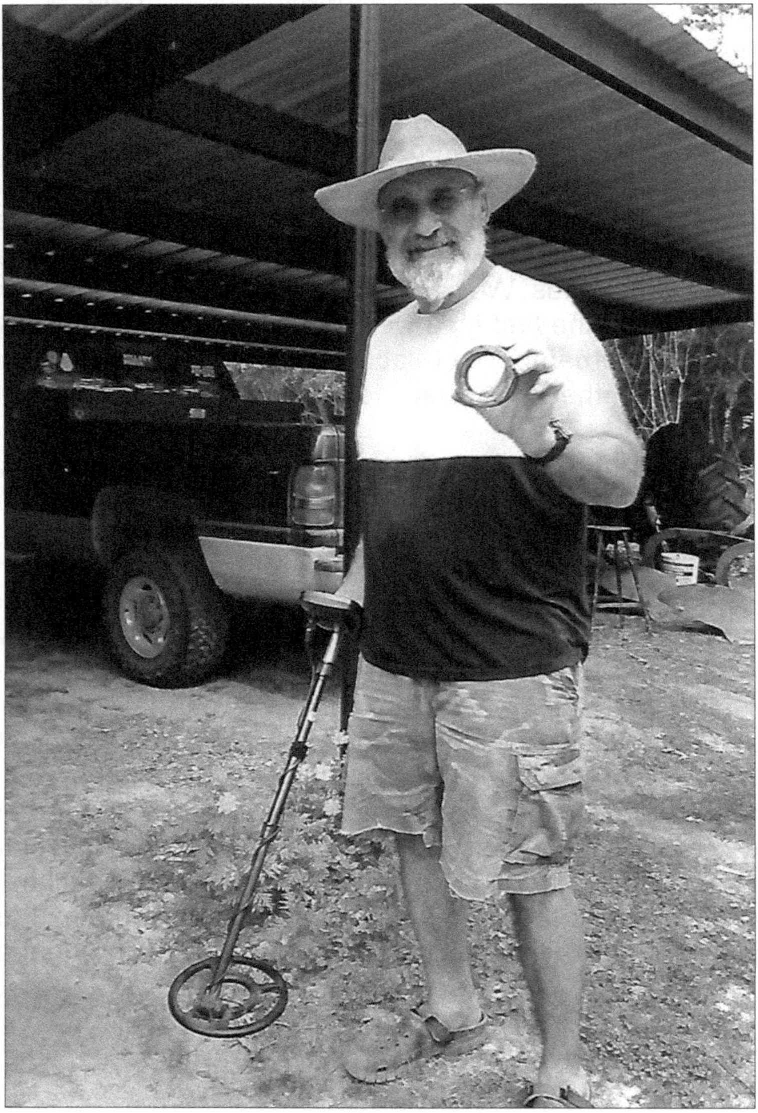

Unexpected Catch

My son gave me a blueberry bush. I planted it in my summer flowerbed. The first year it made eight delicious blueberries for me! The second year it made ten, but I never got any of them. I assumed that the birds got them because they disappeared. Never having grown blueberries before, I was wondering how to care for the bush. I was glad that it had survived, but I wanted it to flourish! I asked for advice from a friend who had grown them before. He said that I probably needed another plant so they would cross pollinate. He also suggested that I move it to a spot that received more sun. So I purchased two new plants. They were sticklike in appearance with the roots extending down in plastic bags. My husband planted them in pots to allow them time to root out and put on leaves before we transplanted them into the ground.

I moved my original blueberry bush to a sunnier spot in a new flowerbed just off the southeast corner of my house. When the new bushes were looking great I transplanted them into that flowerbed near the original bush. They all three grew and looked beautiful! We had a particularly cold winter that year with snow, and temperatures dipping down to 8- or 9-degrees Fahrenheit. We hardly dip into the twenties in our usually mild winters. This cold spell lasted for several days and affected many plants, not to mention the tremendous water pipe damage and electrical power grid failure. It was labeled a disaster in our state. My original blueberry bush did not recover. The two new bushes, however, survived and in about a month looked great, each putting on blooms and then berries.

To keep the birds from stealing my tiny berries I purchased some bird netting. It was fourteen feet long and fourteen feet wide. I cut off a piece ten feet wide and left the fourteen-foot side alone. Bill helped me find some metal sign posts to secure in the ground for supporting the netting above the blueberry bushes. The metal signposts were four feet tall and looked like huge croquet wickets. I also had a five-foot-tall tomato cage that we put around the tallest bush to help support it. The area we covered with the netting was about five feet by three feet, with netting highest in the middle draping downwards over the signposts on down to the ground. The extra netting at the bottom I rolled under on the ground and set a few heavy rocks around on top of it to secure it. I didn't want any armadillos getting under! I had stretched the net tightly between the supports so no birds could simply push the net in to get my gorgeous blueberries. The netting worked great! My berries were enjoying the sun on their way to maturity.

A pair of house wrens decided to build their nest in my begonia basket which was on the opposite end of the front porch. It was near the kitchen door, an area we frequented. They worked faithfully and built their large nest to one side of the hanging basket. I was carefully watering the plant from the other side of the basket as they worked. Before too long three eggs appeared and the female started sitting on them. Every time that my watering nozzle first moved the leaves she would fly out and perch in the nearby crape myrtle and carry on with all sorts of anxious chirping until I finished watering all the plants on the porch. Then she would return to her begonia basket nest.

We were thinking, "That is really pretty smart thinking to put your nest there." We have bird nests around the yard every year: cardinals, blue jays, wrens, etc. Many of them hatch the eggs and then nature's "food chain" "disappears them." In the woods near us we have owls, raccoons, and nonpoisonous snakes that are the possible culprits. I know it is nature's way of balance, but I still feel sad anytime I find a fresh nest which has had eggs or fledglings, all of a sudden empty with only a few eggshells and feathers left behind. I am always pulling for the mama birds. I guess it is that motherly kinship. The begonia basket eggs hatched, and the wrens were busy all day every day feeding those little mouths.

One morning Bill went out and as he walked back into the house he said to me, "There is a snake caught in the bird netting, right on the ground. Looks like a milk snake."

"What?? Is it dead?"

He walked back out. I rushed out to look. It was a strange sight – a milk snake with its head and neck about eight inches into the netting. I ran to get my shovel to touch it and be sure there was no motion. Then I retrieved my gloves and went a little closer. I knew that I had watered the blueberries sometime in the last two days and the snake was not there then. The shovel couldn't pull the snake loose. It was definitely caught. Reluctantly I touched it with my gloves. As I pulled it I could see there were two large milk snakes! Large to me – they were more than two feet long but folded up in the netting! Then I saw something else! A large copperhead snake was under the other two! Three snakes were caught in the netting. The copperhead was not as long as the other two. I jumped back even though they were dead. I had to be sure. Bill helped me check – there was no life at all. It was a really weird sight. It looked like the snakes had had a party or maybe a rescue mission gone awry! Just for my own satisfaction I pretended this was the copperhead that two years earlier had bitten me and slithered off. (That account is written in the second essay in this book entitled "Life is SO SWEET.") I had finally gotten him! Well …. maybe it was him, maybe.

Bill went to the garden, and I was left to get the snakes out of the netting. Their skin seemed so thick. I touched it with my bare hand. It felt smooth and tough. I put my glove back on. I pulled but the snake would not come loose. If I chopped with my shovel to get them out it would totally destroy the bird netting. (Hold your breath now and don't throw up!) I wound up getting my large utility scissors and cutting them into eight-inch pieces, one snake at a time. Then carefully removing each piece from the netting. It was a gruesome task, but there was no liquid. It was like cutting durable soft plastic. (But very gross. I am a brave girl, I'd say.) I got them out.

Why were the snakes so near my house? I had not even seen any snakes in a year or more. And here there were three! The next night I flipped the light switch on, opened the back door, and walked out to see a huge rat snake lying across the back of Bill's chair near my dining room window! This thing was like three feet long and its head went up. Startled, I darted back inside screaming! The thing was looking straight at me through the window. His eyes were shining, and he looked aggressive. Byron, who had recently moved from the Northeast United States to the country, grabbed his camera and took a short video of the snake as Bill went out the door.

"It's just a rat snake. For Pete's sake calm down!" Bill said to me as he closed the door. I was still shaking.

Rat snakes are not poisonous snakes. They eat chicken eggs and bird eggs and small rodents, but I have heard of people receiving nasty bites from them. At the sight of Bill the snake lost his intimidating boldness and slithered off.

Then it dawned on me! Bill's chair was roughly six feet from the hanging basket which held the wren and her babies! There was a decorative tea cart next to Bill's new white wicker chair (that Tracy Schulke had picked out and delivered to me), but the back of the chair was the tallest thing around that was even remotely close to the baby birds! The rat snake was trying to get the baby birds! That hanging basket had been a smart selection for the nest.

Each morning after that I hurried out to listen for the baby birds chirping. They were always quiet until the momma bird moved the begonia leaves as she flew in. Then they started hollering, "Feed me first!" "Feed me first!" "No, me first!"

We were planning to have a get together at our house for Memorial Day. Every day I was checking the birds to be sure they made it through the night and also watching the netting at the opposite end of my long porch. I thought, "The last thing we need is a snake caught in the netting." That would freak out the guests and sort of ruin our party, putting everyone on edge. So every day I checked for snakes, a freaky thought! Sure enough I found another dead milk snake in the netting and got it removed before the party.

The following week the wren was still happily feeding the babies! Success! One by one the little wrens flew out of the nest – all on the same day! They had made it.

That was months ago and I have not seen any more snakes. My conclusion is that the snakes were being drawn by the bird nest, a potential meal. But, perhaps they just wanted my blueberries.

When we installed the bird netting I never anticipated this interaction with nature, but the netting did its job and more! None of my blueberries were stolen. They were delicious and the wrens are singing as they forage among my flowers.

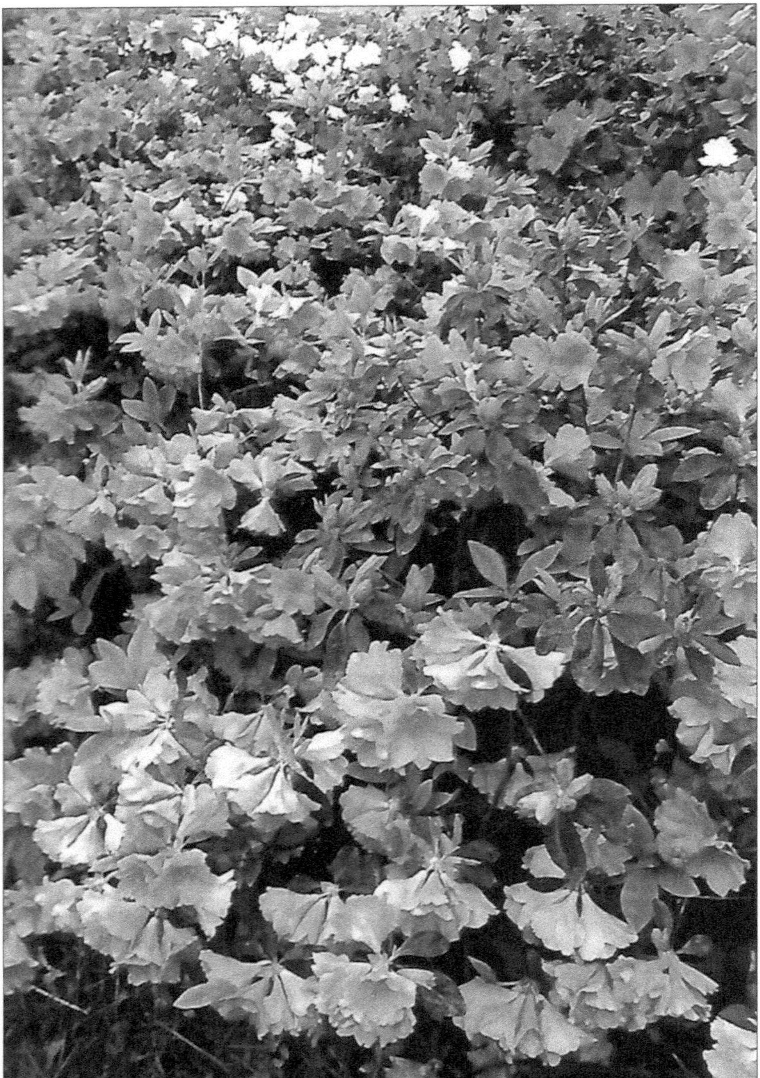

I Recommend Jesus

By Sarah Muñoz

When life's going good, when life seems sad,
I recommend Jesus.

When life's at its start, when life's at its end,
I recommend Jesus.

If you've lived well or made mistakes,
I recommend Jesus.

There's no one who doesn't need Him.

If you feel well or if you are sick,
I recommend Jesus.

If you feel safe or if you're afraid,
I recommend Jesus.

When you're at ease or suffering much pain,
I recommend Jesus.

There's no one not loved by Him!

If you have enough money or if you are poor,
I recommend Jesus.

If you are lonely or have friends galore,
I recommend Jesus.

When life seems on track, or if your train has derailed,
I recommend Jesus.

We all need a Savior. He's the only one there is.

His blood is sufficient to cleanse all our sins.

He knows all our trials, has felt all our pain.

You have nothing to lose, eternal life to gain.

We can be saved if we call on His name.

He offers forgiveness. His pardon is great.
I recommend Jesus.

He demands first place in our lives; it's what He deserves.

His arms are open wide to big and to small.

He only refuses those too proud to call.
I recommend Jesus.

Alice - "in Wonderland"

Being retired and living in the country one sometimes becomes friends with the oddest of God's creatures. For instance, I had a large round thermometer on the porch. Bill had secured it on one of the white square columns. The thermometer was a little bit larger in diameter than the side of the column where it hung. Therefore, one could see behind it if you looked from the correct angle. There was a tiny green tree frog that lived back there. Occasionally at night he would attach to the window of the back door and easily catch tiny bugs which were attracted to the door by the light shining inside the house.

When that thermometer cratered we got another similar one and there was always one, sometimes two, tiny green tree frogs living behind it! When the newer thermometer quit working we bought a seventeen inch long rectangular one that fit inside the width of the column. It was a very attractive thermometer that we purchased at a Bass Pro store. The paint was gorgeous, depicting a beautiful ten-point buck. At the top was a bust of the deer, a posed close up of him showing off his antlers and at the bottom of the thermometer was a smaller full body painting of the same deer running. The thermometer was beautiful, but it had two major problems. One, the width fit just inside the white porch column and that now made it impossible for the little tree frog to get behind it. So after ten years of having a friendly little green frog on my window pane at night I had to adjust to only seeing the flittering bugs that were attracted to the light. The second problem with the pretty thermometer was that it never worked right! It was obviously off, but it was a great piece of art so Bill acquired a small round thermometer with a magnet on the back and attached it to the painting. Wa! La! Problem solved. Well, not exactly. I still missed the friendly little green frog. But how can you be friends with a frog? I'm not sure, exactly.

I have other friends in the country like the birds that frequent our birdfeeders. We have cardinals, blue jays, titmouse, chickadees, woodpeckers, and doves that come to eat all the time and others like finches that are seasonal. The birds don't come directly to me, but they will frequent the feeders when I am on the porch or in the swing. As long as I am still, they are content. When one of the feeders is empty and I go out to fill it, my feathered friends start chirping to share the good news before I am even finished. So, I do have some interaction with the birds. The owl sounds friendly as he "who whos," but I know he is looking for dinner. That's not a friendly sound to the small animals. They scurry to take cover.

The pesky armadillo is not really a friend. He can be destructive. But I do have interaction with him. At least he mostly stays outside of my little flowerbed fences. He sure tears up the yard at times.

The bunny is cute, and I enjoy seeing him on the edge of the yard eating grass. Sometimes I see him under the birdfeeder. It makes me think that I am "Alice in Wonderland" when I see the squirrel, the bunny, and the birds eating together. Last year there was a bunny that seemed to stay under the maidenhair fern about 20 feet from my front door. But the extreme winter weather we had froze that fern down to the ground and the bunny moved elsewhere. Thinking back, the first flowerbed fence that I put up was because the bunny was chomping away on my flowers. Yes, I like him on the edge of the yard.

In 2000 Bill's brother-in-law John welded him a stationary "boot scraper" for Christmas. It is a piece of metal art and stands 33.5 inches tall. Each metal rod side has a horseshoe near the bottom with a 12-inch bristle brush attached. It stands on a round base that has an 18-inch diameter. The "boot scraper" sits on the porch and on muddy days Bill can rub the bottom of his boots across the brushes to clean mud or dirt clods off before he comes into our house. It is decorative and very useful for folks who love the outdoors and trek around in it. The eighteen-inch diameter mounded metal base is actually an old farming disc from a tractor implement. It has a one-inch square hole cut out in its center where the axle of the implement fit through. When the paint job began to look faded, I decided to move the heavy piece of art off the porch so I could repaint it. I leaned it to one side to sort of roll it and was surprised to see a large toad sitting under it! I was surprised that he could fit through the one-inch square opening to get in. And how could he hop out? I am not sure, but after I completed the paint job and returned the "boot scraper" to its spot I started checking under it periodically and, yep, the toad would be there!

I have a unique cement planter. At one time someone poured cement around the 7 by 7-inch base of a square pole to make it stand alone. When no longer needed, the pole was taken out, so the cement mound is like a nine inches tall planter having an uneven bottom. It sits straight but the uneven form allows a bit of room at the bottom. I discovered that the center (where the pole was) would hold a five- or six-inch potted plant so I made it into a planter. I trade the plants out seasonally and the appearance is that the plant is growing in a rock. The five- or six-inch pot hangs around the center hole leaving 3 or 4 inches of space below. The toad discovered it to be a perfect summer home! When I water my plant a bit of water always drips to cool his area down below. Because of the uneven bottom the toad can get in and out at will. I accidentally discovered him down there once when I was changing out the plants. Now I occasionally see two large toads down there! It's a nice cool spot on hot days. Sometimes if I turn on the porch light and go out at night the toad will be sitting in front of the windowed door watching me. I have credited him with catching mosquitos when it is rainy and damp. It seems that he helps me control them.

The friendly toad is under the "boot scraper," in the cement planter, sitting in front of the kitchen door, or maybe in the front flowerbed. If he is in the flowerbed he always hops out when I water. I find it interesting that he likes the moist coolness but doesn't want to be sprinkled! I have also credited the toads with catching the mosquitos that come by the front door. That makes them very beneficial friends.

One morning I went out to clean off a long spider web that I could see outside on one of the long windows by my front door. I took my broom and got the spider web down. Then I noticed a bit of dirt and started sweeping the cement porch. I saw a dark brown spot and thought, "I don't remember the porch looking so dirty." Then farther down on the porch I saw two more spots with red blood and (this is gross) a little strand of internal organs stretched out to be about four inches long! I had never seen anything like this on my porch before. Something had wrestled with a smaller critter and evidently eaten it. There were no feathers left behind, so it probably was not a bird that got consumed. Because of the blood I thought that maybe it had been a mole. They are a little bigger. Looking around I saw that something had dug through the rocks in my French drain beside the porch revealing a gopher's hole or maybe a mole's tunnel. I thought I had found a tiny foot, but it turned out to be a shred of a piece of bark from the azalea bed. There was no evidence of fur left behind; there was just that little strand of internal organs. I couldn't figure it out!

Later when I watered my flowers, I noticed the flowerpot was removed from the unique cement planter and was lying on the ground with some of the potting soil knocked out or dug out of it. Although disturbed, the purple pinta flower, which had been currently residing there, was not broken. Before I put the pinta back I looked into the planter – no toads! My heart sank. As I continued to water I found on the other end of the porch another smeary dark spot where there had been a struggle. Also I saw that something had dug in one of my flowerbeds. Bill was gone, so when he got home in the afternoon, I was anxious to find out what he thought could have happened. After all, he grew up in the country. Surely, he would know.

He said, "I have no idea."

Me, "But the internal organs are so small. Probably not a squirrel."

He said, "Maybe it was a toad frog."

Me, "Looked too long for that." I had not thought about a toad. I was thinking it was a mole.

Bill said, "No, since they were stretched out it could have been."

I was sad. I still couldn't figure it out. There were quite a few armadillo signs in the yard, but how could an armadillo have done this? A five-gallon planter had been dug in. An armadillo more than likely could not have stood on his tail to reach that high. It seemed like it could have been a dog chasing toads or going after a gopher. And there was the digging in one flowerbed. But there were no dog prints. Maybe an owl did it, or a raccoon. And where were the toads? Were there several eaten, not just one? It seemed like too much blood for one toad.

A little later I asked Bill to tip the "boot scraper" over so I could look underneath. Yes! There was a toad. He was safe under the metal disc dome!

The next morning everything looked pretty calm, but then I noticed the pinta pot! It was squashed in and lying sideways in the cement planter. Once again, the plant was not broken. Some critter had also dug in another five gallon planter! This was a beautiful coleus. The plant was leaning to the left but had not been broken. Why was something digging in my pots? More evidence! The rocks were dug out at another spot in the French drain revealing two small tunnels belonging to either a gopher or a mole.

"It looks like something is looking for gophers." Bill said.

"Or toads." I chimed in. I straightened the purple pinta. There were no toads underneath.

My day was pretty busy so it was fairly late when I worked on redoing that area of the French drain that had gotten messed up. I took up all the rock, filled in with soil, put down landscape plastic that generally goes under bark in a flowerbed to help discourage weeds from growing. It is porous and water passes through it easily. I put the rocks on top of the landscape plastic. I was using it to keep the rocks in the French drain from sinking into the soil as quickly. It was starting to get dark and suddenly I was surrounded by a jillion night sounds! I turned on the porch light and to my delight the toad pushed his head up through the one-inch hole in the base of the "boot scraper." Amazing! How could he even reach that high? I went to the cement planter and three toads had their heads peeking out between the flowerpot and the cement edge! Wow! It seemed that they were holding onto the edge with their tiny front legs. As I watched they somehow pulled themselves around and up into the pinta pot. Then they hopped out onto the planter's cement mound and then hopped off toward the loud sounds of the night. The toads were okay! Happy me!

Two days later I was surprised to again find things amiss when I went out to water my plants. Bill's friend had brought him five flats of starter plants and Bill had left them near the house for easy watering. These were seven-inch-tall cabbage and broccoli plants planted in six packs with six of the small packs in each flat. As soon as I went out the kitchen door, I noticed that the flats were moved and some of the six packs were knocked out and lying on the ground. One was upside down. I surmised that something had been chasing a toad or toads! What was this critter that kept coming back to my yard? Another of my five-gallon flower pots had been dug in. This one was a periwinkle with hot pink blooms. The plant was leaning a bit but was not broken. What animal could reach up into my taller planters to dig? Maybe it was a coon.

I ran to look! The cement planter with the purple pinta was not bothered, but there were no toads underneath. I checked under the "boot scraper." I was excited to see a toad sitting there! For several days I continued to check under the pinta. There were no toads. I thought that maybe whatever had ransacked the starter plants had gotten them.

I noticed that the area of the French drain which I had redone appeared lower in one spot and two mole/gopher tunnels were exposed on the edge. I decided to again redo that area. I took out the rocks and rolled back the landscape plastic. Suddenly I noticed two little legs flash out of one tunnel and then disappear again. Hmmmmm. I went inside to watch through the window before I proceeded. I was fairly sure this gopher/mole tunnel was old, and I had planned to put moth balls inside before I covered it. But if the toad was living in there, I would not do that! As I observed from the window, I saw a toad come hopping through the azalea bed. He shimmied down the bigger rock that was on the edge of the French drain. The tunnel openings were just below this rock. The toad sat facing them. He sat for a moment, then hopped toward the one on the left and peered at it; then he hopped before the other one where I had seen the tiny feet come out. He was very still. Then slowly he proceeded into the tunnel. Either my toads had moved, or this was another happy toad home!

As I finished redoing the French drain, I purposely leaned rocks covering the toad holes against the bigger rock.

I was careful not to fill them with dirt or cover them with the landscape plastic. I was so happy that the toads had survived the assault!

I so wanted to know what had chased them. I knew the armadillo had been in the yard but simply could not imagine him being able to get up into my large pots. (That's a funny picture). I put my Canary home security camera up on the porch at just the right angle, but the night was uneventful. I set up the outdoor trail camera a few times, but there was no motion detected. All seemed calm for a week or two, but then the unimaginable happened! One morning there was again blood on the porch! Many rocks in the French drain were moved. A major scuffle had occurred. And then I saw it! Finally, there was proof! There was a paw print in the blood on the porch. The critter terrorizing my toads was a raccoon! We set two traps and waited.

Ah, sweet! We caught the raccoon! I was really missing my toads. There were none under the pinta in the cement planter, none under the "boot scraper," none in the flowerbed, none watching me through the door. I got up early one morning, turned on the living room light, and went to the piano. I started playing a soft tune. Momentarily I noticed motion on the windowpane. There was a small green tree frog! He was a little larger than the ones that used to live behind the porch thermometer. It had been a few years since I noticed one of these at my window. He shimmied up about 12 inches. Then he stopped. Maybe he was listening to my music! His belly was against the glass, and I noticed that his throat was moving. He stayed there until my song was finished. Then he was gone. He must have been singing along! After all, my name is Alice......and folks do "wonder" about me.

finally a "Paw Print" – a raccoon!

Expectations

I am a good one for wanting to help. I like to volunteer to keep my grandchildren occasionally so my children and their spouses can have meaningful refreshing times together without the children. As the older grandchildren grew, I liked to have them help me with the little ones for overnight fun or week-end adventures. It worked out great. The littles had fun, the older grands enjoyed their cousins, Bill played with the grands, and I played with kids too, but was able to spend time in the kitchen preparing food and snacks for everyone! And I also had time to clean up the kitchen.

So, I planned one such adventure. "Let me know which dates will work best for you," I said. Well, the dates that worked best for them happened to be three days after the Opening Day of deer hunting for bow hunters! That meant that Bill would have other things on his mind. As a matter of fact, his brother invited him on a hunt/work trip. His brother had had surgery on his shoulder and needed help with a few things. Not only did Bill have other things like hunting on his mind, he also had other places! I generally go along on the hunting trips, and we usually stay from Friday until Tuesday. This time I had other plans and could not go. Bill gave no scheduled dates for his trip. It was a last-minute invitation and could be as long as ten days (or more). Okay. Even though Bill would be gone, I could still do my adventure with the littles! Maybe the older grands could help. The littles would come on Wednesday and stay until Saturday evening.

As it turned out the older kiddos had other responsibilities like school and schoolwork on their schedules. No one could commit to help me. Oh, my! I mean, I raised four kids. I taught Sunday School and Children's Church for years. I taught the nursery, well, I taught every age group at one time or another over the years. I potty trained my four littles. I taught public school for years. I also taught college kiddos.

"Surely I can do this. I am a great team player! (But there was no team, just me!) The grandkids are good kids, but I am getting a 'bit older.' My energy might run out."

I've always tried to not take advantage of people. I consciously have tried to not assume others would do certain things. And I surely never volunteered Bill for things without asking him. Yet, in the back of my mind I guess I had some expectations. I guess I was thinking there would be someone to help me. I have helped a lot of people, so I thought I had "planted good seed in this area." I have been there for others many times so I thought someone would be there for me. Ephesians 6:8 (KJV) says, "Knowing that whatsoever good thing any man doeth, the same shall he receive of the Lord, whether he be bond or free." Okay. It doesn't say how you will receive the help. I thought, "I guess God is going to give me energy and wisdom (especially energy) to do this myself since there is no one to help me." I changed my game plan. I planned meals that were faster, easier. I bought new puzzles, new crayons. I figured that I would be the number one playmate (the only one) so I prepared for it.

Inside, I felt abandoned. How can you feel abandoned when you belong to the King of the Universe? It happens when you are looking to others instead of looking to Him. I expected others to love the adventures, like I did. I have helped them so many times! "Don't let bitterness creep in," I reminded myself.

As I prepared for the littles, I prayed quite a bit. I was excited, but still felt abandoned. One of my Facebook friends posted a sermonette about a rattlesnake bite. The piece said that it is not the bite that is life threatening; it is the poison. Life is full of bites. You just gotta' make sure the poison doesn't linger. "Speaking right to me," I reasoned. Another friend posted, "See things as they are, not how you want them to be." Hmmm. I, girl of faith that I am, am usually "speaking things that be not as though they are." It is a delicate balance here, but I got it: Face reality. Another FB friend posted, "Every night forgive those who hurt you, pray for those who need it, thank God for everything you have." Hmmm. Why were my friends preaching today!?! No funny stories, just serious lines. I got it. As I continued to pray, in my mind I saw my mom standing alone and singing from the bottom of her heart, "He's all I need. He's all I need. Jesus is all I need. He's all I need. He's all I need. Jesus is all I need!" Growing up I had seen Mom sing this many times.

I started singing it. It had been a long time since I had felt that I had no one to count on. I should have been praising God for that fact! But I wasn't. Tears were flowing and I felt abandoned. I kept singing. In my mind I could see the expression on Mom's face. The words of the song were powerful, and the sweet presence of the Holy Spirit surrounded me. Now she was singing the verse, "He's wonderful! He's marvelous! He's God's only son! He wants to do a work in you – a new work in you!" And then I sang the chorus again, "He's all I need....." I started feeling it. I started believing it. "I CAN do this! One way or another we will survive!" Yes.

I was very happy when the kiddos arrived. We played inside, we played outside, we ate, we threw caps up in trees! While trying to figure out how to get the caps out of the trees I got an unexpected text from Bill. "I am almost home. See you soon." And just as my energy slipped away, he did get home. He easily reached the caps out of the trees! While I cleaned the kitchen he read stories, said prayers, and put one kid to bed. He read more stories, said more prayer, and put the second kid to bed. Together we read stories, said prayer and put the third kid to bed. God did make sure I had what I needed!

Before I went to bed that night, I looked briefly at Facebook. A friend had posted an Irish Proverb, "A good laugh and a long sleep are the two best cures for anything." I laughed at myself. My Heavenly Father had more than repaid the good I had planted. Then I got another unexpected text! One of the older Grands had made room in her schedule. She was going to come help me play with the littles on the weekend! And she did.

> "Knowing that whatsoever good thing any man doeth, the same shall he receive of the LORD, whether he be bond or free." Ephesians 6:8 (KJV)

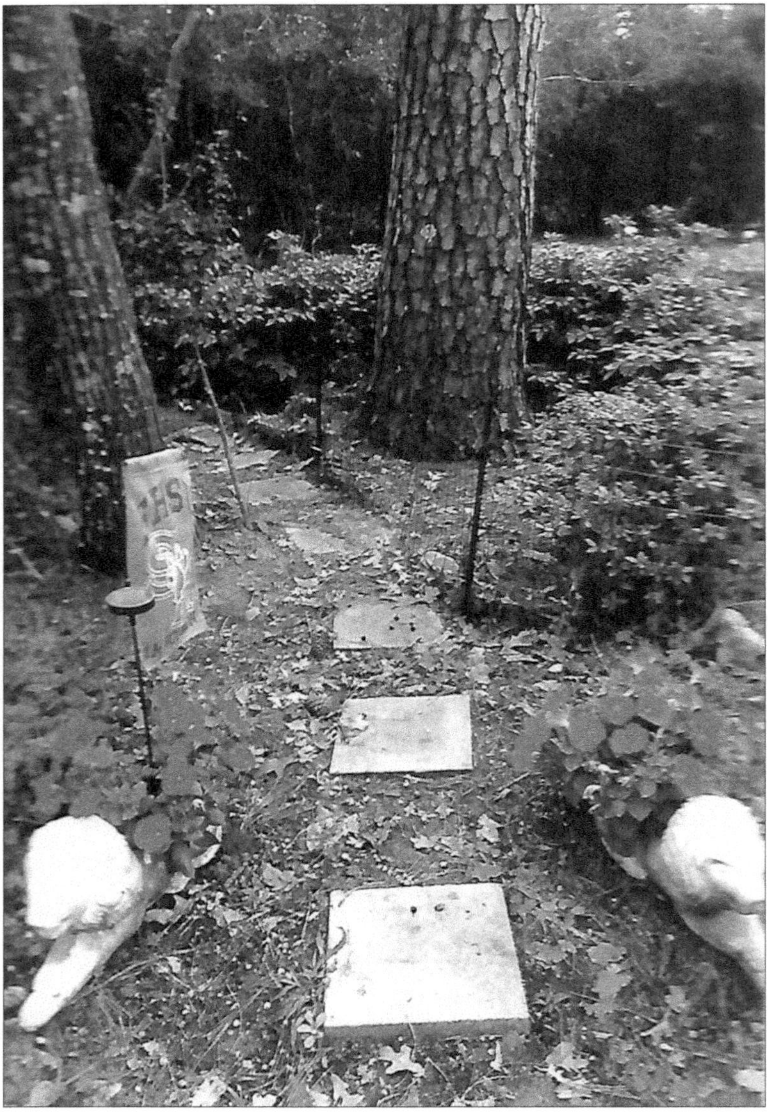

High Praise

High Praise

God, I come to you this morning
My melody is new
I sing to glorify You
Your presence settles like the dew.

It's then I realize…
My life's the melody You long for
It's the praise that never ends
It's like a concert in Your garden
May You hear a perfect blend.

Let my life be a song of worship
Let my life be a song of praise
As I humbly live it for You
Let others see Your mercy and grace.

My life sings to You
As I maneuver through my day
My life sings to You
As I pause and kneel to pray.

May my sour notes come less often
Let my rhythms remain true
May the loud and soft parts punctuate
This song that rises up to You.

My life's the melody You long for
It's the song that never ends
Like an aria in Your garden;
May You feel this song I send!

"Friendly" Law Enforcement

I love the Blue.

Oh yes, I respect the law officers. I respect them, cautiously. As a kid I never had much contact with law enforcement officials. Romeo Lewis was our friendly law officer in Somerville, Texas. My older sister worked for him at the City Café and I saw him on occasion when we picked her up from work. He was courteous and always waved to my sister and me if he drove passed us around town. He knew that I was one of the Hein girls and I knew that he was the law.

When I went to Caldwell to take my driving test at age 16, the young officer there was a very friendly fellow. All was going well until I had to demonstrate my parallel parking skill. Now, I had done it numerous times in practice successfully. I pulled up beside the vehicle in front and was nervously turning the wheel and slowly backing into the spot. All of a sudden there was a loud BAM!!! My mind was thinking, "What did I hit? That car was several feet away." I quickly adjusted and pulled out which messed up my alignment with the parking spot. I stopped. The officer began laughing very loudly. My dad's red and white Chevrolet Impala that I was driving had no air conditioning, so our windows were rolled down. The officer had banged the outside of the car door with his fist! Now he was laughing, uncontrollably, about it! It was impossible for me to correct my blunder. We drove back in silence. Almost there, he turned to me and said, "You failed the test." I tried to control myself and focused on the road, but he saw the tears forming in my eyes. "Just kidding!" he replied, "I was only teasing you. Hey, I'm just kidding!" He tried to make me smile, but I was uptight. We arrived back at the courthouse and when I opened the car door to get out, he said to my Daddy who was waiting for me, "If you want to see this girl cry, all you have to do is tell her she failed a test." He laughed again. "Let's go inside and get her license completed." I got my license that day, but I was totally deflated and humiliated. First, I didn't make the parallel park and second, I didn't realize it was a joke! Serious me.

Well, I took law officers seriously. I was a law-abiding citizen and, therefore, I felt that the law was on my side. Years later, living in another town, I was stopped for some small driving violation and the kind officer gave me a warning, not a ticket; so, I received the mercy of a lawman. (Of course, I was much younger and blonder in those days. I'm not sure if that had anything to do with the mercy I received.) But that mercy re-enforced my thinking that lawmen are our friends.

Fast forward to an older me with three grown kids and one younger child still living at home. It was Christmas Eve and my third child had just returned from Florida. He had graduated our local high school with honors, had gone off to college, and had worked very hard and completed his degree in three years! He was about a month into the great job he had landed and was home to the town he loved, the town he grew up in. He was a kid who was smart and well liked. His classmates had voted him to receive the senior class scholarship. Not a lot of money, but a great honor, because his classmates had selected him. He flew home to Texas and his girlfriend drove down from Austin where she and her mother now resided. She was also a graduate of our local high school and was also excited to return HOME. They went to Walmart for a few items and as they were leaving, they noticed the new park across the street. They drove over, parked, and walked the trail, finding a small pond.

My phone rang, jolting me awake. I sleepily said hello, but woke up quickly when my son said, "Mom, we are at the jail."

"What?" I had not yet met this girl.

"Mom, we are at the jail. We were at the new park by Walmart. We were sitting on the pier talking. A policeman walked up and said, 'This park closed at 10 PM. You are breaking the law and I will have to check your licenses.' He accused my friend of having an unpaid ticket and took her to jail. She has to pay $500, or she will have to stay in jail until Tuesday."

"Until Tuesday!! What about Christmas?"

"He doesn't care that it is Christmas Eve. He is talking to us like a jerk. When he saw my out of state driver's license he started pouring it on. Do you have $500 she can borrow?"

"Five hundred dollars! I don't even know this girl. I can let her borrow it, but if she doesn't pay it back, you will have to pay me. I don't have $500 to throw away."

"Mom, I know she has the money. She has been saving for a computer. I know she has the money. She will pay you back."

"Did she call her parents?"

"Her mom is working the night shift. She is a nurse in Austin. (Austin is three hours away!) The phone number for the hospital is in Bethany's phone in her purse, but they won't get her purse for her, and they won't let me see her either. The officer said that he ran Bethany's license plate number, and it shows an unpaid fine. Bethany said that when she bought this car and was driving it home, she got stopped. There were expired plates on the car at that time. But she told this officer that she already mailed in the fine payment a while back. He won't listen to her."

"Alright, I will bring the money."

I hurried to get dressed. I got the money and drove to the jail. Bill stayed home with our younger child who was sleeping. I met my son, and we went inside and walked up to the window at the counter. Where was the Mr. Rogers' neighborhood friendly policeman, you know, the kind, caring officer? Where was he when you needed him? I recognized this policeman. No, I hadn't met him, but I had seen his picture in the paper before. He had received some type of award locally. Maybe this was our lucky day!

Christmas Eve! Wow! He scowled at us. That was a shock to my limited knowledge of law enforcement.

I said, "We have the money to get Bethany out." I presented it toward the small opening under the glass.

He leaned back. "I can't accept cash. It has to be a money order."

"What do you mean it has to be a money order?"

He said it again, "I can't accept cash. It has to be a money order." He stood up and started walking away from the window.

I said, "Hey! Where can I get a money order this time of night?"

He turned back around. "Well, the Seven Eleven Store has them."

"Thanks. We'll be right back."

We made it to the Seven Eleven Store before midnight, and the girl behind the counter said, "We had them, but we are all sold out. I sold our last one earlier."

I tried to stay calm. My son was getting very annoyed. We drove back to the jail. The officer again scowled at us.

"They were all sold out. Where else can we go?"

He looked at me like I was nuts. "Go to a bail bond store."

"Look, I don't even know what that is. I have never had anyone in jail before. Where do I need to go?"

"There's a bail bond place in the Woodlands. There's also one on FM 1960." He gave us the addresses. I'm thinking, "So this is what parents go through when their kids get in trouble: middle of the night trips to the bail bond store."

We took off again. It was an eerie feeling, driving around in the wee morning hours looking for a bail bond store and thinking, "This is where the law breakers go."

Christmas Eve? What if Santa saw us out and about?!

We found the first bail bond store, but it was already closed. Christmas Eve hours, I guess. Time was passing.

We drove to the second place. There was one car parked in the parking lot and a guy was in it. He stared at us. I assumed he knew that people came here with cash to get money orders. Surely he knew I was carrying some cash. I could see a paper flapping on the front door of the dimly lit building. I got out and walked to the door methodically. I was aware that the guy was watching me. It was a heavy door without a window. This place had no windows. The paper taped on the door had these words: "I had to run an errand, but will be back."

"You are kidding me, right!" I am thinking. Out loud I said, "We will wait."

I walked back to the car, got in, locked the doors, and we sat. After thirty minutes or so the bail bond guy returned. He unlocked the heavy door and we hurried in behind him. He was not friendly, and he did his business in this dingy place behind a window with bars. But he had what we needed. Yes! We got the money order! We drove back to the jail.

The officer seemed unhappy to see us. This was no longer the wee hours of Christmas morning. It was Christmas morning. He took our payment and went to get Bethany. When he walked her out she was shaking. This beautiful young woman, shaking. No one had told her we were getting money to help her. In her mind she was having to stay until Tuesday, December 27 like they had threatened. No one got her cell phone so she could call her mom. They wouldn't get her purse so she could take her medicine. Yes, she was shaking. We hugged each other. She, so happy to be out of the cell, hugged me. I was finding it hard to believe that they never told her help was coming; now my tears were flowing. I hugged her. How could they be so heartless? Especially on Christmas! She was still shaking. Noticing that she was barefoot I asked for her shoes.

"No, she can't have them yet. She won't get them until she gets in the car. We can't risk her running away."

What? I didn't even have time to process this nonsense! She had paid to get out already! My brain was numb. I was just happy that we were getting out of this nice "friendly" neighborhood place.

And so Bethany walked barefoot on the cold December ground. The officer followed carrying her shoes. When she sat down in the car, the officer handed her the shoes. We said goodbye and she drove off to her friend's house where she was staying on this trip.

My son and I set out for home. When we got home it was around 5:00 AM. Merry Christmas! I was still shocked at the rudeness exhibited toward us. These two young adults had experienced quite a welcome HOME.

Before 10:00 o'clock that morning Bethany was at my house with the $500. My admiration for this girl swelled. She'd had almost no sleep, but she took care of her responsibility. She said that she was going to appeal the charges. The court date would be in January.

"Please let me know when it is. I want to make sure you tell the judge that they wouldn't let you get the phone number to make a call and tell the judge that they wouldn't let you get your medicine. It's outrageous!"

I haven't had any more jail experiences, thankfully! Oh, how I wanted to write a letter to the local paper. This was unbelievable! The only thing that held me back was knowing that there might come a time when I needed police assistance. I didn't want to be marked as trouble. So I just processed it as "live and learn."

Bethany never told me her court date. She made the three-hour trip from Austin and appeared before the judge by herself. Turns out she had mailed the payment for the fine to the wrong address. It went to another county. She said that she got all of her money back, except around $70.

What a hometown welcome that was! What a lesson that Christmas Eve! Yes. I respect the law, cautiously.

Do I hate the police? No. Does Bethany hate the police? No. Do I support the "Defund the Police" movement? No. Shortly after I wrote this piece a wave of hatred for law enforcement swept through the big cities in the United States. It trickled down to the smallest of towns with criminals demanding rights and politicians supporting the law breakers ahead of the police. Many police were killed. I almost did not include this essay in my book because I did not want to appear anti-police, but it did happen.

Parents get frustrated having to correct their children over and over. Suppose you were the police, and your job was to correct the worst behaved humans. Suppose you had to constantly deal with criminals, haters, and instigators. It would wear on you. Behavior like what happened to Bethany is never excused, but it is the exception, not the norm. Just like all teachers are not mean, all mailmen are not irresponsible, all doctors are not greedy, and all coaches are not grouchy, all police do not feel obligated to "break you down."

Funny thing, the Pastor my church hired about three years ago is a retired city of Houston police officer! I am definitely seeing another side of the "policeman." I respect the Blue, even if they disappoint I respect what they stand for. I appreciate what they do in our communities. I am thankful they go to work each day.

It was Christmas morning.

Hidden Treasure

When I was young and standing on the precipice of my future, God spoke to my heart that I should attend Midwest Bible Institute, a small Bible college in Webb City, Missouri. I had worked hard in high school to earn my spot as Salutatorian (2nd highest) of my graduating class. I had also won first place in writing competitions – first in UIL (University Interscholastic League) district competition and first in UIL Regionals in Texas. Those honors netted me a full scholarship to Blinn Junior College, a full scholarship to Texas Women's University, and a full scholarship to any state supported four-year university in Texas that I chose – University of Texas, Texas A&M University, Texas Tech, Sam Houston State University, University of Houston, etc. But I distinctly felt God impress me to go to Midwest Bible Institute, fondly called MBI. How could this small school influence me or shape me better than the universities?

It didn't make sense to me. I wrote a letter to the UIL board asking if I might postpone use of my scholarship for one year. I was thinking that I might go to MBI for one year and then return to attend the university. The return letter I received said that I must use my UIL scholarship in the fall of 1971 or I would lose it. My dad said, "If you take off to that school in Missouri we are moving there." I was his tenth child. He had been through many children leaving home, and he was not anxious for me to go. I couldn't shake the feeling that God wanted me to go to MBI so after much prayer, I gave up my scholarships and sent my application in to MBI where I would have to find a job to stay in school. My summer job had allowed me to save enough money to cover my first semester.

In August I received a letter in the mail informing me that Midwest Bible Institute had moved to Houston, Texas. Houston, Texas! It was a little more than an hour from where

I grew up. My dad was relieved; college no longer involved a move to Missouri. A few weeks later I was settled in my dorm! The giants I found there who profoundly influenced me were Rev. Earl and Ruth Pruitt and Rev. Paul Allen and Bonnie Pletcher.

I had met the Pletchers and had become close friends/pen pals with their daughter Janeva through Onalaska, Texas Summer Youth Camp. At MBI most students attended church in Houston. I wanted to go to Deckers Chapel (now Living Stones Church) in Decker Prairie, Texas. The Pletcher family of eight had decided to go there and they invited me to ride with them. Yes! During those rides we became close friends, and my destiny was in the making. I met a tall, handsome, nicely tanned guy named Bill at Decker's Chapel. None of us realized the miraculous move of God's Spirit that we would get to be a part of in the next few years.

One day Janeva Pletcher came to visit me at my dorm room. She said, "My dad thinks you shouldn't bleach your hair. You should be what God has made you to be. Don't be fake." I, a natural blonde all my life, was floored, shocked, insulted! I was almost speechless, but I managed to explain it to her. Looking back now it is funny, but I didn't laugh then. After Janeva left, I cried. Most people had always liked me; I was Homecoming Queen, Yegua Princess, Most Likely to Succeed. I was bruised, but I got over it. (Proverbs 25:12 in the Message Bible – "... and a wise friend's timely reprimand is like a gold ring slipped on your finger.")

When Brother Paul Allen saw that I was sincere he and I became good friends. He had a great laugh! He loved to beat you in ping-pong or outwit you in some class discussion and then laugh about it. (It reminded me of my older brother Hugo beating me at checkers and then doubling up with laughter.) I could take it! I didn't have much time for ping-pong anyway. Between classes, homework, KP chores (not that much, really), I was working at J.C. Penny's in Northwest

Mall. Brother Pletcher even picked on me in class. Right in the middle of Holy Spirt class or Daniel/Revelation he would say, "Do you want to see Alice blush? She is going to blush. Just look at her." He would laugh his little giggle, the class would laugh, and I would blush. It was pointless for me to try not to. I tried to smile. We were great friends.

In Missions class Brother Pletcher, a former missionary who had lived in Mexico more than ten years, said, "If you are blonde and God sends you to Mexico be careful. Be aware that in the mountain villages that I went to any blonde was elevated and sometimes worshipped. It was so rare for them to see a blonde they treated one as a god. Don't mislead." Wow! I'm special! I know that's not what he meant. I got the point.

When campus was closed for Christmas and I needed to work a few more days, he and Sister Bonnie allowed me to stay at their house. They had four teen-age girls and two younger children. They were like family. They were there when I completed my two-year Bible degree and Bill completed his Christian Worker's degree. And, yes, they were there when Bill and I got married. Janeva was one of my bridesmaids. We went to the same church as long as Brother Paul Allen taught at MBI. The church grew from 40 to around 350 people! He counseled the church leaders, did bus ministry, taught Youth Sunday School, and served on the Church Board. When we outgrew our facility he moved his class to the church bus, the blue one. He found the mover who came from Pampa to help us with the larger facility. He was all about reaching people for Jesus. His birthday was the same as my mom's. On and on and on, we were connected in big and small ways. Then they moved away. But their influence was permanent.

Bill and I visited the Pletchers in their home in Pampa, Texas the week of August 18, 2014. He was a bit frail and moved more slowly, but we reminisced like old friends do. We are thankful for this giant God placed in our lives.

The other couple that profoundly influenced Bill and me at MBI is Brother Earl and Sister Ruth Pruitt. What giants in the earth, what kingdom builders they were! Brother Pruitt was Superintendent of Midwest Bible Institute when we attended there. In Bible College if a guy asked you out you had to get permission from Brother Earl before you could go! He had this dry sense of humor, and I could never tell when he was joking about Bill and me going out! So I made Bill clear our dates (even though I lived on campus and Bill drove from home)! We also had rules that you had to double date! So much fun we had. Jackie Crabtree and Freida Booth were our regular double dates in '72-'73! We became lifelong friends!

Brother Pruitt was a gifted Bible teacher. I was trying to think which of his teachings influenced my life the most. His Bible teaching was superb, and he kept me wanting to learn more. But his "Stewardship" class and his "Christian Home" class taught me how to live successfully. Bill and I both have been blessed in our home because of him. He taught that marriage is not 50-50. Marriage is 100-100 and don't worry about keeping track of your spouse's tally, keep your own up there! He taught that man is the head of the home, but his wife Sister Ruth said, "Yes, but the wife is the neck that turns the head!" Besides leading Bible College Brother Earl pastored in several states and profoundly influenced the world with all the pastors he trained and ordained. When he later returned to Texas, we saw him occasionally at various church gatherings. He was always friendly and kind to us. In 2012 he came to Living Stones Church to do a Sunday School teacher training for our teachers just because I asked him. He was one of the first people to buy my first book <u>Nora Mae, a Remarkable Insignificant Person</u>. He was an important guy in God's Kingdom, even serving as President of the Full Gospel Evangelistic Association for several years. I can't even name all the important roles he has had, but I am so thankful that I got to be friends with him. He and Sister Ruth visited our home.

These two spiritual giants, Paul Allen Pletcher and David Earl Pruitt that God had directed me to when I was eighteen years old, died within a few months of each other. Brother Earl died in June of 2021 and Brother Paul Allen died in September of 2021.

I graduated from Midwest Bible Institute in 1973. God never sent me to Mexico except to visit my little sister who did become a missionary, but years later God did impress me to go back to college and get my Bachelor and Master degrees. My MBI foundation is one of the treasures of my life. Listening to God when He impressed me to go to Midwest Bible Institute brought great dividends. In Matthew 13:44 Jesus said that the kingdom of heaven is like a treasure hidden in a field. For joy over it one goes and sells all that he has to buy the field. Listening to God's voice and trading the scholarships I had for a Bible education helped me find the greatest treasures of life.

"Let it Flow"

That day I was searching for the perfect gift. There were a few "hot" toys at the time, toys that were extremely popular. One such item was the "Cabbage Patch" doll. Stores ran out of these pricey dolls. They had no more in stock.

I was shopping and there were no more "Cabbage Patch" dolls on the shelf. My little girl wanted one, but it had taken me too long to get my money saved for Christmas shopping. We had three children and our family was on a tight budget. We didn't do without, and our bills were paid, but extra cash was hard to come by, particularly in December.

We owned and operated a retail plant nursery – Schiel Nursery. We sold plants and related products and my husband Bill designed and did landscaping. December was usually our slowest month of the year for sales. Trying to maintain their own family budgets, most people were not landscaping their yards; they were spending money on Christmas gifts for their families this time of the year.

Finally having my money together, I had gone to our local Walmart to shop. There were no "Cabbage Patch" dolls. None. Zilch. Zero! "Cabbage Patch" dolls were cloth dolls with a plastic head and hair made of yarn. I managed to find a kit for sewing and stuffing a cloth doll. The doll had a cloth face, but the hair was made of yarn. I had learned to sew in Homemaking class in high school and had sewn many items for myself and kids clothes for my kiddos. I knew that I could do it. I put the kit in my basket. (I did sew the doll and an outfit for her before school let out for Christmas. It wasn't a "Cabbage Patch" by a long shot, but it was the best I could do. We did manage to get a "Cabbage Patch" doll the next year.)

As I continued shopping that day, I put a few more items in my basket with the doll kit. The store was quite crowded. Some people were on edge because the "Cabbage Patch" dolls were all gone. (Santa was having problems here.) I turned and reached to get an item from a top shelf. Out of the corner of my eye I saw an arm reaching into my shopping cart! A woman was trying to take an item from my basket! I turned quickly – my shocked face was on level with her face. She dropped the item and took off around the corner. "Really? I have got to get out of this store!" I reasoned. I headed for the long check-out line.

And so that next year I did my shopping earlier. I started saving earlier – as I could. I did not want to be in the late Christmas shopper crowd. As "Black Friday" shopping became a popular thing I never participated. "Black Friday" is a shopping day which is the Friday after Thanksgiving. Many stores announce huge sales that day – dropping prices low. They also extend their business hours. It is called "Black Friday" because retailers who have been operating "in the red" all year finally make a profit. Their operating accounts move from red to black. They count on Christmas shoppers to keep their businesses going. "Black Friday" quickly became the official start of Christmas shopping. People began to arrive earlier and earlier to be at the front of the line to get in. They wanted to make sure the biggest and best items were not out of stock when they moved through the front door. I never participated in the frenzy.

Years later I was teaching school. Teachers have to plan to have time for extravagant things like shopping. School was getting out for Christmas break on Friday and Christmas was the middle of the next week. One of my teacher friends named Renee commented, "I can't wait to finally go shopping!"

Another teacher commented, "You are kidding, right? It's gonna' be a mad house."

I was all ears as Renee answered, "I love shopping this time of year. I love being a part of the crowd! I love feeling the hustle and bustle, the excitement of everyone buying surprises for their family and friends!"

I was amazed! I loved this attitude! "I need to get out there with a different attitude," I told myself. And so, although my shopping was mostly done, I went to the store to feel the excitement of the hustle and bustle. I liked it!

I recalled a sermon that I love by the late Dr. Bill Stephens of Merced, California. He had a series of messages entitled "Success in Life." One of the sermons in the series was "Who I am in Christ." He taught that we are the temple of the Holy Spirit. I Corinthians 6:19 (KJV) "What? Know ye not that your body is the temple of the Holy Ghost which is in you, which ye have of God, and ye are not your own?" The Holy Spirit dwells in us. Dr. Bill also said that God's river of life can flow through us. John 7:37, 38, 39 (KJV "In the last day, that great day of the feast, Jesus stood and cried, saying, 'If any man thirst, let him come unto me and drink. He that believeth on me as the scripture hath said, out of his belly shall flow rivers of living water.' (But this spake he of the Spirit, which they that believe on him should receive: for the Holy Ghost" was not yet given; because that Jesus was not yet glorified.)" If we believe on Jesus, the Holy Spirit is flowing through us – as we live on the earth. Dr. Bill said, "When you enter a room let it flow. You don't have to say a word. Just drown them with God's love flowing from you."

Okay! So I began to try it! I'm still doing it! In a crowded store as I walk among the shoppers I smile. If a baby's crying, I smile at the mother, "It will get better." If someone bumps my cart to move me over, I just smile and move over. "Merry Christmas!" I say again and then again to another stressed out shopper. It seems to remind them why they are shopping. In a long line I strike up a conversation, "Isn't it great that so many people can afford to buy gifts for their loved ones?" I always say, "Merry Christmas" to the person working the cash register or the one monitoring if it is self-check. "Thank you for being here today putting up with all of us." I smile and smile. In my head I can see it – the river of God's Love flowing from me to them.

If I hear someone very irritated, I try to go stand nearby, perhaps on the next aisle and silently pray for them – when I come around the corner with a soft "Merry Christmas" I almost always get a smile. I've seen scowling faces light up as they return my greeting. It is a simple easy way to diffuse tense moments. It is enjoyable to help change a stress filled atmosphere to a joyful one.

You must try it! Let it flow!

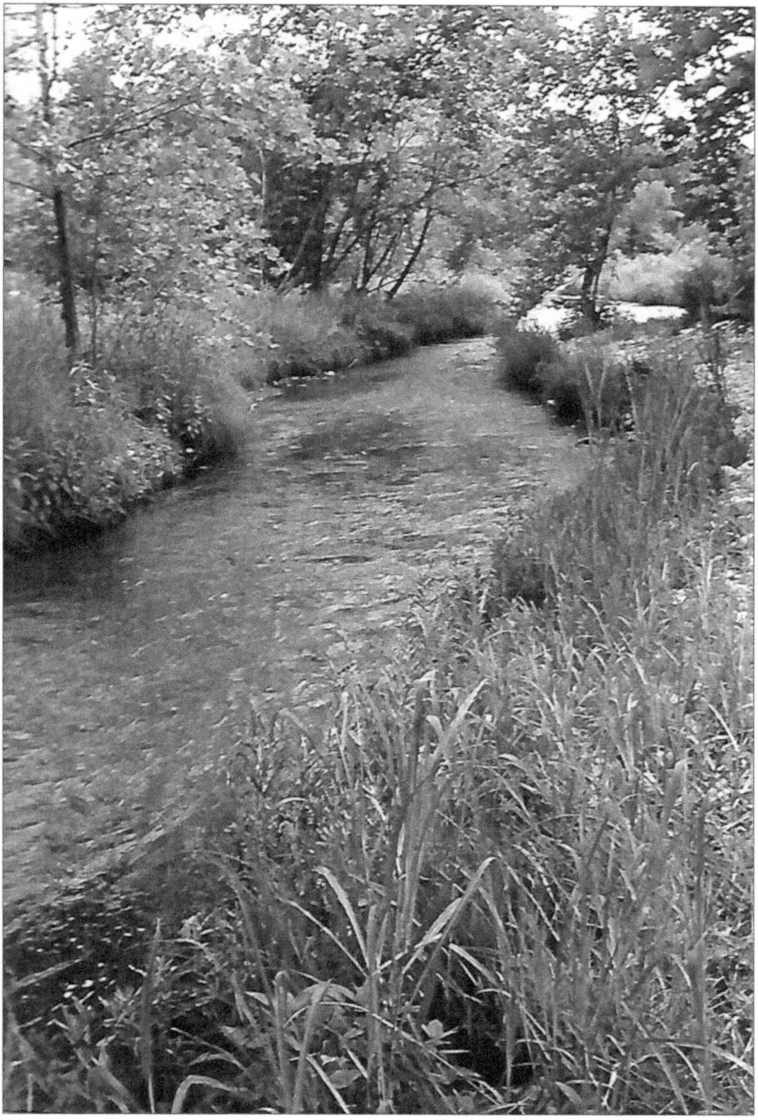

Preach It!

I feel the preach coming alive in me this morning. Hang On!

"Thou shalt not bear false witness against thy neighbour." The year is, well scholars are not sure of the year, but it is recorded in the book of Exodus chapter 20, verse 16 (KJV). Moses was on Mt. Sinai receiving the Ten Commandments from Jehovah God. This is categorized by theologians as commandment number IX. Pretty important stuff! "Thou shalt not lie."

And it gets more serious. This statement is recorded in the last book of the Bible: "But the fearful, and unbelieving, and the abominable, and murderers, and whoremongers, and sorcerers, and idolaters, and all liars, shall have their part in the lake which burneth with fire and brimstone: which is the second death." Revelation 21:8 (KJV)

As twenty-four-hour news became more popular in our society the importance of fact checking a story before reporting it waned. The race was on to see who could report an event first. There was no time to check out its merit. As this happened more and more "news" was reported incorrectly. Blatantly false stories became the norm with no obligation to retract them or correct the inaccuracies. Even the airports chose to run 24-hour news and many a lie was broadcast proudly. Does this change the fact that God said, "Thou shalt not lie"? Of course not, but even reporters viewed as having integrity began to insert their own opinions along with the false narratives. To save "face" they never apologized except rarely.

Actions surrounding the 2016 election in the United States made it seem that lying is no big deal. The Democratic National Committee paid the former British spy Christopher Steele to manufacture evidence against Donald Trump in the form of a dossier which was later found to be lies. The lies were only discovered because of a court order. James Comey, the then director of the FBI, denied knowing who paid for the Steele dossier. Emails from a year earlier proved that he knew all along. How was he accountable? Comey received a lucrative book deal. In 2021 Special Counsel John Durham's investigation verified that indeed the dossier was composed of rumors and lies which Hillary Clinton's campaign and the media knew.

Congressman Adam Schiff, heading up efforts to impeach President Donald Trump, opened one inquiry session reading an entire page of lies about the President to Congress and it was done in front of TV cameras. Those cameras were blaring those lies into the homes of Americans and around the world. The page he read was all lies, but Schiff didn't care. He never withdrew it or corrected it. When pressed by concerned members of Congress, he dismissed them simply saying, "It was a parody."

In 2019 video was released of an encounter on the steps of the Lincoln Memorial. The Washington Post ran the story accusing Florida teenager Nick Sandmann of mocking Native American activist Nathan Phillips and blocking his path. Television station CNN did seven stories on the incident without checking out the facts. NBC also broadcast the story. The longer video revealed that activist Phillips had actually approached Nick. Nick won a lawsuit winning millions for this inaccurate reporting.

Also, in 2019 actor Jussie Smollett lied to the police about being the victim of a hate crime. He falsely reported that he had been attacked in Chicago. He said he had been punched in the face, had had a substance poured on him, and had a rope put on his neck. He also said that his attackers were wearing MAGA hats (supporters of President Donald Trump wear these hats). He suggested that his attackers were white. In December of 2021 Jussie was found guilty of lying to the police and wasting police time and money. Investigation had proved that the hate crime incident was a hoax and Smollett had paid the two men to "attack" him. When he received his sentence in March of 2022, with his fist raised this actor continually shouted out, "I am not guilty." He is currently appealing his sentence.

Listening to TV in January of the year 2022 AD one would think the words of the Ninth Commandment were never spoken. Even the President makes claims that are not true. He recently said that 95% of schools are "back" since the Covid pandemic. But what does "back" mean? At this time classrooms in the Northeastern US still have masked students in desks with Plexiglas shields separating them. The students hear their lessons on online tablets which are sitting on top of their desks. A masked teacher is in front of the classroom behind a Plexiglas shield teaching through a Zoom App on the computer. It is very misleading to say these schools are "back." The President also claims he is responsible for the lowest unemployment rate in the US in years. But analysts know that the only reason the rates appear low is because many people refusing to return to work have been removed from the work force data. With popular opinion turning against him and mid-term elections looming large in 2022, the President finally acknowledged in his February 2022 State of the Union speech that children should return to more normal school.

The President's Press Secretary Jen Psaki reported that Florida did not open their schools in a timely manner after the Covid pandemic. Governor Ron DeSantis contradicted her statements stating that Florida's schools had opened two years earlier and that at that time he had been criticized for allowing students to attend school "in person." When given the facts, Psaki didn't back down.

Recently, one of TV network CNN's spokesmen said, "We will always continue to report news and correct our mistakes." Really? When have they ever corrected their false narratives?

Jolt yourself! Lying is not acceptable even if it seems to be the norm in our culture. It is deadly.

> Ephesians 4:25 "Therefore, putting away lying, each one speak truth with his neighbor, for we are members of one another."
>
> Proverbs 12:19 "The truthful lip shall be established forever, but a lying tongue is but for a moment."
>
> Proverbs 12:18 "There is one who speaks like the piercings of a sword, but the tongue of the wise promotes health."
>
> Proverbs 19:5 "A false witness will not go unpunished, and he who speaks lies will not escape."
>
> Proverbs 19:9 "A false witness will not go unpunished, and he who speaks lies shall perish."

When Paul wrote about the armour of God that empowers us, he recorded in Ephesians 6:14 (KJV) "Stand therefore, having girded your waist with truth, having put on the breastplate of righteousness,"

Pursue truth! Teach your children to be truthful. God's words on the subject are more powerful than mine!

> John 8:32 (KJV) "And you shall know the truth, and the truth shall make you free."
>
> Paraphrasing John 14:6 - Jesus said to Thomas, 'I am the way, the truth, and the life. No one can come to the Father except through Me.'

Wow! I think that covers it. When preaching, God's Word is the best reference. This is not a little matter. Be truthful.

Wait! There's more!

> Proverbs 3: 3, 4 (KJV) "Let not mercy and truth forsake thee: bind them about thy neck; write them upon the table of thine heart:
>
> "So shalt thou find favour and good understanding in the sight of God and man."
>
> Proverbs 6:16-19 lists six things that God hates. Lying is mentioned twice: #2 – a lying tongue and #6 – a false witness that speaketh lies. The passage gives a seventh thing which is described as an abomination to God: "he who sows discord among his brethren."

In the book of Jonah chapter 4, verse 10 God refers to the 120,000 citizens of Nineveh as people who "can't tell their right hand from their left." We sure have a lot of people in our society who can't tell lies from truth. They can't tell right from wrong. With all the political games being played by the politicians and the unreliable news reporting, things can get pretty twisted. Be sure you digest the following point! Throughout history God has always been faithful to keep those who follow Him, those who trust in Him, those who study and obey His Word. If we keep close to God, we have no need to fear. His presence will guide us. Jesus said, "My sheep know my voice." He guides those who acknowledge Him in all their ways. Rest in Him. Embrace the truth. Be bold! Take action! Vote against those who embrace lies.

That's it! The preach is over!

Tranquility

Election 2020 – Fraud?

It's hard to believe Biden won!

There are plenty of questions, Maud

I am disheartened by what he's done.

His propaganda work is bold.

Misinforming, dodging all questions

Over and over same lies told

He's hoping for a mass delusion.

Truth has a permanent abode.

It doesn't compete with trendy lines.

Solid rock truth never erodes.

When lies wear thin like gold truth shines.

On Day 1 he changed border law.

Did away with orderly entry.

Seeing chaos, feelings are raw.

Border patrol crushed by policy.

Masses illegally crossing

Crowding in shelters become sordid.

This President, facts a' tossing,

Ignores the cries for help of hundreds.

Big cities were looted and burned.

Congress gives them millions for wasting.

City mayors? Their heads they turned.

Tyrannical gin they've tasted.

In midst of all this upheaval

I remember Isaiah 9:6

"Government is on Christ's shoulders"

Giant relief – is it His to fix?

We must let Jesus give us peace.

That inner calm - our minds it defends.

Verse 7 gives this tranquil feast:

"of His peace there will be no end."

Jesus said, "My sheep know my voice."

Prayerfully, his leading you must note;

Following whatever His choice;

Should you run for office or just vote?

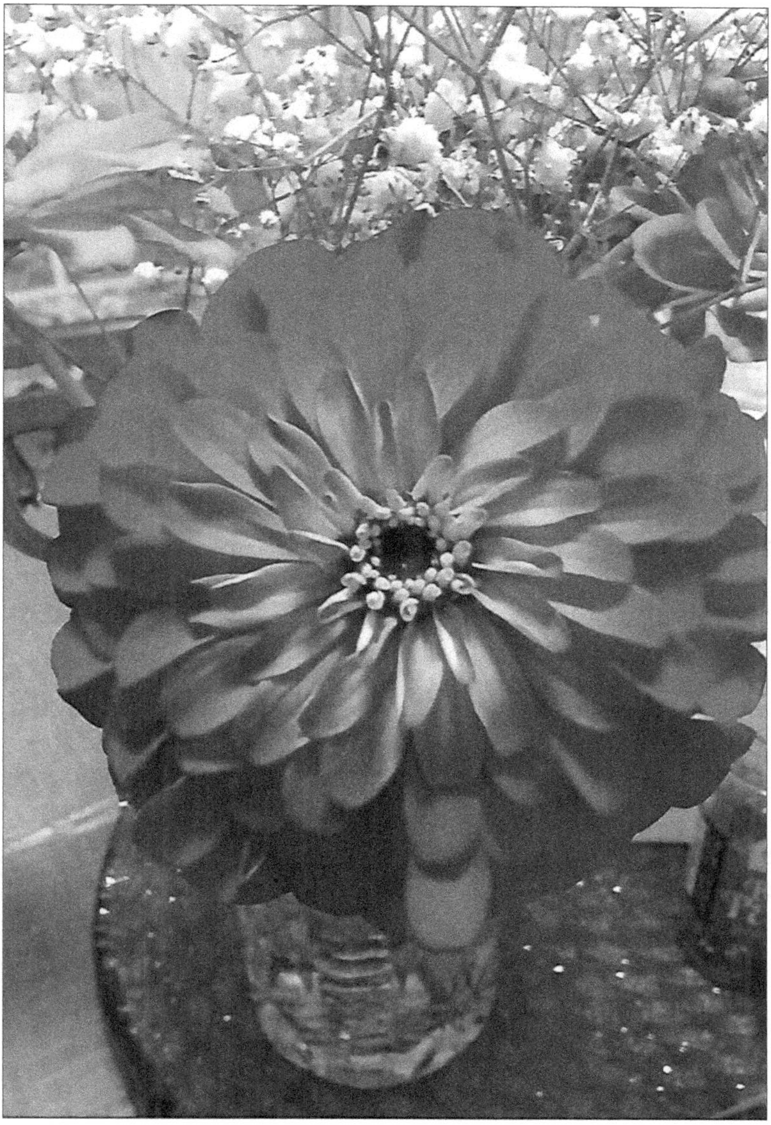

"Clothes Make the Man" (or Woman)

In August of 2018 we took a vacation trip to Mount Rushmore. That was our destination, but we visited other states on our way to and from South Dakota. Our ultimate goal is to visit all 50 states in the U.S. We drove through Oklahoma, Kansas, Nebraska, and Iowa. Bill was totally intrigued by all the cornfields. We stopped to take pictures of the cornfields. We followed signs to a Garage Sale in the middle of the cornfields so Bill could talk to the people who knew all about them. (And I purchased a belt and some tiny angel salt and pepper shakers which I love.) We were in the "Breadbasket" of the United States!

Leaving Iowa we traveled to Walnut Grove, Minnesota (Yes! We did the tour!) and northeast through the outskirts of Minneapolis on into Wisconsin. I was searching for curds! You know Wisconsin is famous for cheese. I had met a Wisconsin native at the Walmart in Tomball, Texas about four months before our trip. She had told me, "You gotta' eat the curds there! A trip to Wisconsin is nothing if you miss the curds! They are so scrumptious!" So, I was searching for curds; I didn't really know what I was looking for. Was it kin to cottage cheese?

All I knew about curds was that Miss Muffet in the Nursery Rhyme had eaten them!

"Little Miss Muffet

Sat on a tuffet

Eating her curds and whey.

Along came a spider

And sat down beside her

And frightened Miss Muffet away."

Yep. That was the extent of my knowledge of curds. So, I looked it up and found that when milk sours it separates. The coagulated part is the curds. The liquid part is the whey. So Miss Muffet was eating soured milk. Soured milk? Oh well, we drink buttermilk, we eat cottage cheese, we eat cheese. I wonder what Miss Muffet was wearing.

We stopped at a lot of shops in Wisconsin looking for souvenir coin purses for my collection of coin purses. We asked for curds everywhere we stopped. Finally, we were directed to a refrigerated package of curds that were to be heated in the microwave! Okay! We conquered! We could hardly wait to try them at the hotel that evening. Ugh! They turned out to be sort of mushy with little flavor. Not very impressive! I collapsed on the bed thinking, "This is not the curds experience that I was expecting! Was there something wrong with the lady's taste buds?"

The next day as we were planning to leave northern Wisconsin by driving across Lake Superior into Duluth, Minnesota we unexpectedly found some curds in a little shop. We had stopped to walk along the lake shore. The curds were presented in brightly colored snack packages! Maybe! We excitedly paid the cashier and dashed to the car. We were not disappointed! These curds were similar in texture to soft Cheetos cheese puffs. They were very flavorful and must have been the curds the woman had told me were to be sought after! Our trip to Wisconsin was validated, after all. Lol.

I didn't find a souvenir coin purse in Wisconsin. But early on in a little boutique on the town square in Chippewa Falls I had found a small burlap zippered pouch. "If I can't find another one, this will work!" I bought it. Printed on the pouch are the words "Dream without Fear." We continued to look for a coin purse, but this one was it! The pouch is now proudly displayed with my coin purse collection.

While in Minnesota we made sure to eat a fish called Walleye that had been recommended by a friend. The first one we saw was on the wall of a museum. The Walleye was covered in fur, and it was grinning! It was a prank display in the collection to catch you off guard. Right in the middle of the other beautiful native creatures, was the doctored Walleye. Interesting! At the restaurant we ordered the real thing, and it was as delicious as we had been told. But the image of that furry Walleye grinning at me still lingers.

We drove on, spent the night in North Dakota, and then attended Sunday morning church services with the friendly people there. The next night we stayed in Pierre, South Dakota. We got a great room for a great price! It seems that most tourists don't go to Pierre, they head straight to the Mt. Rushmore area and look for accommodations closer to the attractions. From Pierre we drove west and then stayed in Rapid City. Mount Rushmore was fantastic! Amazing artwork! I was surprised to find it a world attraction. Like Niagara Falls or New York City Ground Zero, there were tourists speaking many different languages. There were multiple other attractions to visit and things to experience in the area.

Quite a few loaded tour buses were coming and going. The driver of our tour bus was delightful. In some places the road passed through dark tunnels in the rock with only an arm's length of clearance on either side of the bus. Vehicles and other buses had to wait to take turns going through. Our driver said, "Watch this! I keep this little sign handy to use when I need it." He put the sign in the front window of the bus. It said, "Student Driver." All of a sudden everyone was letting us go first.

There was a couple on our tour bus that we noticed several times as we loaded and unloaded. They were wearing noticeable cowboy boots and cowboy hats. The woman was wearing a gorgeous turquoise outfit that sparkled with beads and rhinestones and she was carrying a large purse just as attractive.

"They have got to be from Texas!" Bill, who was sporting his boots and jeans, said. (Clothes can speak loudly.)

As we waited for the tour bus to arrive for us to leave Mt. Rushmore, a large crowd of people gathered near the entrance to the attraction. All were waiting on their tour bus. Across the crowd we could see two cowboy hats.

"There they are! Let's ask them where they are from."

We made our way through the crowd and approached the couple. "Are you guys from Texas?"

They smiled broadly, "Yes, we are."

Bill said, "I was pretty sure of it. What part of Texas are y'all from?"

The man answered, "We are from a really small community. It is just north of Houston."

"Really? What is the name of your community?"

The man replied, "We live in Decker Prairie." He laughed, "Ever heard of it?"

Bill smiled. "Yes! We are from Decker Prairie also!"

"You're kidding!"

It turned out that they live one mile from us! So, we drove 2,000 miles to meet our neighbors. Without those clothes we would never have noticed them. The clothes spoke loudly!

We visited the Badlands area before we headed toward Texas. We drove south through western Nebraska. At times we had spotty or no phone service. We were thankful for our trusty Rand McNally Road Atlas! Smoke was blowing in from wildfires nearer the Pacific. We were on a lonely road with almost no traffic and smoke filling the air. We were happy when we reached Greeley, Colorado. Cell phone service returned, and I phoned my nephew. He instructed us where to meet them for dinner. We found the shopping center and were excited to see Jacob, his wife Mindy and their two boys in the parking lot. As we walked into the restaurant people were noticing me. Was it my accent? Am I an unusually attractive old woman? Wait!! Was something unbuttoned?

As we slipped into our seats at the booth Mindy leaned over and whispered into my ear, "Colorado is not the best place to be wearing that shirt." She laughed.

I looked at my shirt. It was classy! My son had purchased it for me in Waco, Texas at TV personalities Chip and Joanna Gaines' shops. Nice looking shirt, I must say.

I was thinking, "What's wrong with my shirt?"

I am blonde. Of course it took me a minute to get it. In one- and one-half inch tall bold letters on the front of my light gray shirt was this message: PLANT LADY. (I am into plants! Flowers, shrubs, etc.)

Evidently "plants" in Colorado has one certain meaning.

Do you get it? See, it's not just me! The whole world doesn't know that in Colorado "Plant" means marijuana. Lol.

The clothes say it all, or not!

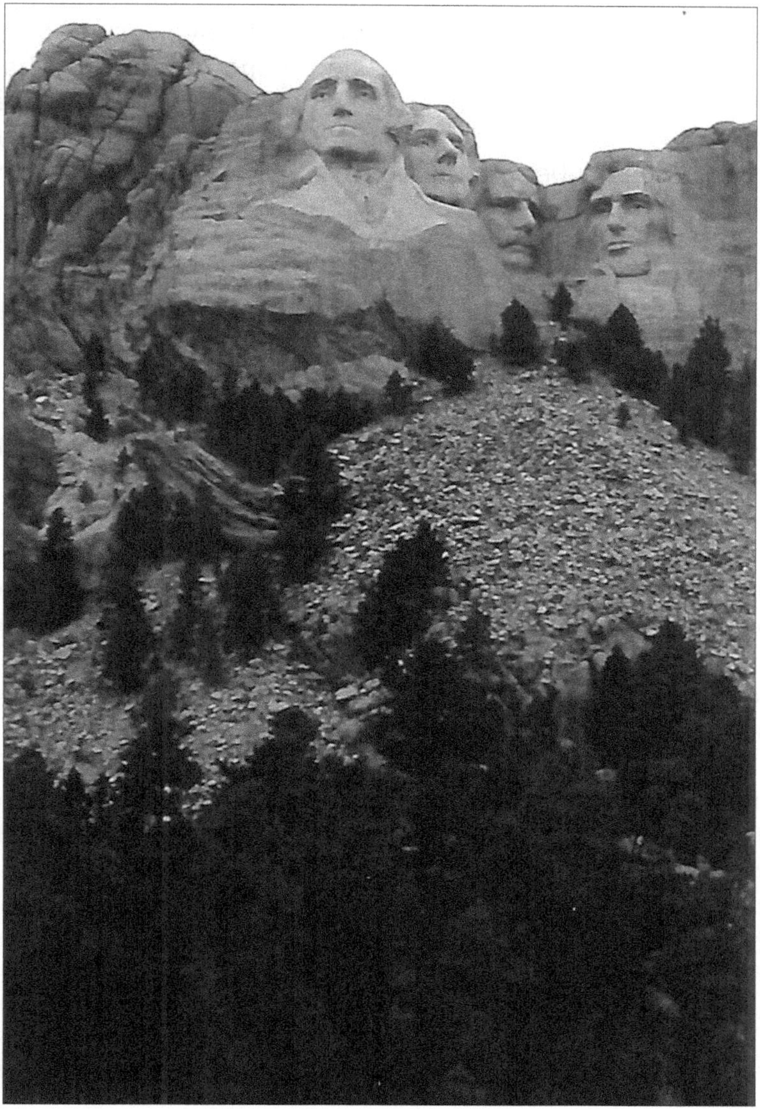

Like a Watered Garden

Looking out the small window I see goats across the neighbor's fence. We are at our friends' river place. I just counted seventeen goats passing along the fence. It has been two years since I have seen any goats in this pasture. A large tree fell back then and broke the fence down, but that has finally been mended. It is very dry here. It is April and there has been no rain this year. The river is flowing because it is spring fed, but the land looks parched. If you walk very far you will see some cracks. Usually everything is lush and green in April. This brown look doesn't generally appear until August's heat zaps everything just before fall cools it down. This year it is as if the bleak look of winter is hanging on. A few of the trees are trying to bud out; many look dead and large branches have broken and fallen to the ground.

The area needs rain desperately. Not too far away wildfires have burned even the grasses. In some places homes have been destroyed. We have prayed for rain. Many people have prayed for rain. Yesterday when we arrived our hopes were high. Rain was in the forecast. A slight cool front was on the way.

This morning we were excited when a light drizzle greeted us outside. It slowly increased until we had downright rain that danced on the roof creating a beautiful sound as drops hit the metal roof. We sat in chairs on the porch to enjoy the rhythm. As we sat drinking in the sounds of the concert my friend exclaimed, "Look at the grass! You can see green color near the ground!"

"I see it too! Wow – green!" I exclaimed.

"Impossible," her husband stated emphatically. "I know rain makes a difference, but not that fast. Let's ask the 'expert' Bill." He pointed toward Bill, "And what do you say?"

Bill glanced around, "I do see green. There was no green before."

"I say you guys are nuts!" My friend's husband blurted out.

I sat there thinking out loud a minute as I offered, "Either the green grass is awakening or the dead grass is getting wet and laying over to expose the green grass that was underneath, but not visible."

"Now that may be or y'all are just nuts!" He repeated.

"Wait a minute," I said. "Look! Just look! Do you know what impatiens are?"

"No."

"Impatiens are flowers whose stems are supported by turgor pressure. When they are needing water they become limp and wilt over to the ground. When you water them, they immediately begin to stand erect as the water is carried to the plant cells. You can see the immediate response to the water as the plants stand. This could possibly be a type of grass that acts similarly."

Seeing his facial expression I added, "It is possible!"

"Y'all are nuts!"

We sat and listened to the rain until the last note. We had received a total of only .3 inch of rain. The birds were singing as if we had had a downpour. We went inside, did a few chores, and ate our lunch. A bit later we went out the back door.

"Look at all the tiny purple flowers everywhere!" Bill exclaimed.

"What do you mean?"

"Just look closely! They are everywhere!"

Sure enough! All throughout the brown frozen, now parched, winter stubs we could see green patches with tiny purple flowers blooming! Everywhere we looked were these tiny purple blooms. The clumps were scattered, but visible. Amazing! Nature had reacted quickly to the small amount of rain that had fallen. One of the basic survival needs that they had been deprived of, had returned. They recognized it immediately. Something within them responded to the life gift.

That's how we are when we acknowledge our Creator. If your heart is parched and dry, or if you feel bent down as a result of the challenges you are facing, the rain of God's presence will lift you up. Something deep within you will begin to flourish. Your heart can sing even in the harshest circumstances.

How do you find it? How does your parched heart and mind receive the invigorating rain it needs?

First, you can read the Bible. The book of Proverbs in the Old Testament talks of this – "The LORD by wisdom hath founded the earth; by understanding hath he established the heavens.

> "By his knowledge the depths are broken up, and the clouds drop down the dew." Proverbs 3: 19,20 (KJV)

> "He shall come down like rain upon the mown grass: as showers that water the earth." Psalms 72:6 (KJV)

In the New Testament this is recorded –

> "That ye may be the children of your Father which is in heaven: for he maketh his sun to rise on the evil and on the good, and sendeth rain on the just and on the unjust." Matthew 5:45 (KJV)

Secondly, you can find the rain that brings spiritual life by going to church services. Isaiah 58:11 (NKJV) "The LORD will guide you continually and satisfy your soul in drought, and strengthen your bones; you shall be like a watered garden, and like a spring of water, whose waters do not fail." All of chapter 58 in the Biblical book of Isaiah is great instruction, exhortation, and promise. Verse 13 (KJV) –

"If thou turn away thy foot from the Sabbath, from doing thy pleasure on my holy day; and call the Sabbath a delight, the holy of the LORDs, honourable; and shalt honour him, not doing thine own ways ..."

In the Message Bible Eugene Peterson interprets Isaiah 58:13 like this: "If you watch your step on the Sabbath and don't use my holy day for personal advantage,

> "If you treat the Sabbath as a day of joy, God's holy day as a celebration,

> "If you honor it by refusing 'business as usual,' making money, running here and there-"

Go back to what your mother taught you, or your grandmother taught you. Go to church. If you have no one who taught you that, do it anyway!

Your whole being will blossom in the presence of your Creator. You will find yourself responding to His voice. You will laugh even though you may have thought you would never laugh again.

Like A Watered Garden!

The Battle of Country Living

Bittersweet! Country living. The past two months the mole and the armadillo have attacked my front yard. This is the first year that the mole has invaded. He usually stays out in the pasture, but this year he has uprooted my impatiens, I don't know how many times, and other flowers as well! The armadillo has been visiting off and on for a few years and it is good to know that he's around. But.... Stay in the woods, please!

Recently the armadillo has visited my lawn almost every night! He's tearing up the St. Augustine grass and messing around in my flowerbeds. He even rooted under my little fences a few times. These are little fences that I put up to help keep the armadillos out of my flowers. The NERVE of this guy. It has become almost a game – each morning I look, "where was he last night?" "how big are the holes?" "did he get in the flowers?" Then, "how can I fix that spot?" I think I finally reinforced the fences enough. Oh, my – staying at home has me trying to outwit the critters! Am I becoming Elmer Fudd? (cartoon character who tried to outwit Bugs Bunny)

On the other hand, I keep thinking, "How is this armadillo helping me? Is he aerating the soil for me? What am I overlooking?" I am so used to my Heavenly Father working all things for my good as Romans 8:28 states, so am wondering, "Is God rescuing me from something that I am not aware of, is He blessing me somehow, or am I supposed to learn something new here?"

A month ago the armadillo did such a mess Bill decided to put the trap in his "trail," which is right off my stepping stone trail. He placed the trap against my "armadillo fence." On separate nights, of course, we caught two raccoons and one opossum! It seems that the critters love my little decorative bridge at the end of the steppingstone trail as much as I do. WELL ... on Saturday night we caught the armadillo, a big one at that! Surprised us! It almost felt like I had betrayed a gaming buddy. Bill relocated him...two miles away. Lol! There are no new holes in the yard this morning, but I am curious if there are buddies. I can't tell for sure. It did rain last night – almost an inch. In the past when it rained much the armadillos stayed in the woods; they are always looking for soft moist soil which is why I had started watering one azalea bed late in the day. That way the azalea bed would be softest, and he would go there – not in the coleus or the flowers! Trying to outsmart his instincts has been very taxing!

Along with the armadillo digging holes, moving rocks, tunneling under my cute landscape fences, and uprooting plants, there is also that mole! And it is a mole, not a gopher; a gopher makes an above ground mound around a hole which leads to his tunnels. The pesky mole tunnels right below the surface leaving a trail of mounding soil wherever he goes. It is hard to tell where the entrance or exit is because the mole seems to stay underground.

As mentioned in my earlier writing, the mole went under my beautiful impatiens flowerbed, loosening soil, pushing up the plants, and nibbling roots as he went. My watering just flattened the soil and left the impatiens sitting up higher with some roots exposed above the ground. The plants began to look very stressed in the August heat. The roots were damaged or out of the soil which made the plants dry out much more quickly. I knew they needed help. I tried adding a little potting soil on top of the exposed plant stems and roots. It didn't seem like enough help for them. They were living and blooming, but not growing into the lush bed full of color that I have grown accustomed to.

I decided to totally replant them! With my trowel I carefully lifted the impatiens, dug holes, and repositioned the plants in the ground, being careful to cover with soil so that when I finished the bed looked nice, like it had been freshly mulched. Gradually the plants began to look healthy and seemed to be establishing themselves again.

But then one morning I went out to find that the blasted mole had come again! He left his mounding trails with soil loosened around the impatiens again! This little beast was ticking me off! The impatiens bed was not the only place he tunneled. He had trails toward the front of my yard and under the trees near my picnic table. He also left tunnels behind the house, beside the house. Maybe there was a whole army of moles! Bill and I planned to go on an eleven-day trip and I was thinking that these guys might totally take over while we were gone!

A friend told me that her aunt always chewed Juicy Fruit Gum and then put it into the mole's tunnels. She said that somehow it successfully got rid of the moles. So, I bought Juicy Fruit Gum. Bill and I chewed it and I put pieces in ten different places in the mole's crisscrossing mounding trails.

About five years ago when a mole was in the vegetable garden, I had purchased some "gopher bombs" (which also take care of moles). I had one of these bombs left over. This was a serious problem, especially since we were going to be taking a trip, so I was going to treat it seriously. The day before we were to leave, I accidentally found an opening to the mole's tunnels in the backyard. Bill had said that if I could locate the active hole, he would put the "gopher bomb" in it. He read instructions online and I eagerly took him to the active hole. We lit the bomb and put it in the open tunnel. As the gases began escaping we covered the hole burying the "gopher bomb" according to instruction. We left on our trip early the next morning. I had high hope that when we returned from our trip the mole or moles would be gone!

These moles are smarter than I give them credit for, or they communicate with and solicit other critters like armadillos to help them out! When we returned from our trip the area by the picnic table where I had put all the wads of Juicy Fruit Gum displayed more mounding tunnels than before. It looked like they'd had a party or invited friends to move in! Grrrrrrr!

Behind the house there were no new trails to be seen. But there were a bunch of armadillo digs. And then I saw it, there on top of the ground, in plain sight, was the "gopher bomb!" The tunnel we had put it in was open. The "gopher bomb" was a few inches away lying on top of the ground. What? Mystery of mysteries! Did a team of moles carry it up there? Did an armadillo dig it out?

Fast forward – one year later – This spring I purchased a mole and gopher sonic spike. I had never heard of such a device before. I just saw it on the shelf while shopping in a local gardening center. It is solar powered and claims to treat up to 7,500 square feet. You insert the spike into the ground and sonic pulses penetrate the soil to repel rodents. No batteries are required. Considering the battle I had with the critters last year, I felt it was worth a try. After four months of having it in the ground turned on I can say that I have had no issues with mole this year! The impatiens that I planted this year are doing fine! They are full of beautiful color and vibrant. There are no fresh mole tunnels in the front yard, none near the picnic table, not even any fresh tunnels in the backyard! I am smiling.

Even the armadillo decided to behave a bit. Maybe he doesn't like the sonic spike either. He has been visiting the yard periodically but has not uprooted any flowers so far this summer. He has minded his manners and stayed outside my little flowerbed fences! I can breathe a little easier and am thankful for the truce, but you never know what will happen overnight. There's never a dull moment with these country critters!

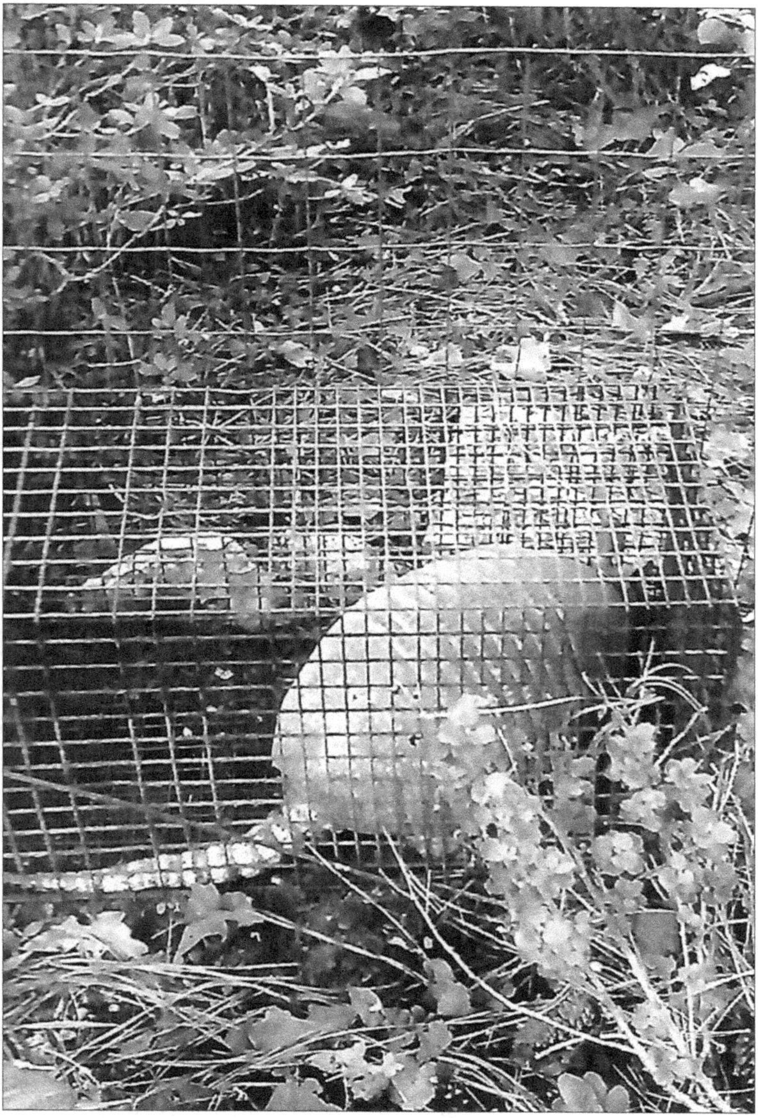

The Best Medicine

There is an old Irish proverb that states that a good laugh and a long sleep are the two best cures for anything. Let's see. That sounds pretty familiar. It should! I have similar words written on a little card that I display on my desk. Proverbs 15: 15b (KJV) "...he that is of a merry heart hath a continual feast." What can we laugh about this morning?

Well, this is a painful laugh, but still a laugh. That counts. About a month ago I was replanting a few plants in my flower bed, the flower bed that has an 18-inch-tall fence around it to keep out the armadillos. Somehow as I stepped over the fence, getting out of the bed, my back foot didn't clear the fence and I fell. Yes, splat! I hit the rock border and the sidewalk but was okay. I am sure that it was quite a sight, me falling over the fence. Only my pride was bruised. "Can't I even lift my leg anymore?!" I blamed it on the shoes I was wearing. They are an old pair of slide-on sandals. Originally, they had a strap in the back to keep them on your foot, but they are old! And that strap has been totally stretched out for a year. Sure, I intended to get new knock around shoes for working outside, but the ones I purchased are too good for knocking around in. Know what I mean? I have rubber boots, but in the summer they get too hot too fast so I only wear those if I am going into tall grass. I have hiking boots, but those are too cumbersome for just knocking around in. Plus, they have strings that you tie, and to untie every time I go inside for something is too much trouble. I have old tennis shoes, but then I would have to wear socks; and those have the string issue too. I have some nice crocs, but I certainly do not want to get dirt in those. I wear those inside! You can see my dilemma. So, I opt for the old slide-on sandals with the stretched-out strap that dangles in the back. I know the shoe had to have slipped and caught the top of the fence. I know that my thought process and the muscle response involved in lifting my leg are not impaired! Not yet! I am not that old! I got up and checked my limbs: all intact! The top of the fence was mashed down. With quite some effort, I was able to straighten it, covering my blunder, and did not mention it to Bill.

Earlier this week, the armadillo got under the fence of that flower bed! Pesky guy. He kept on until he found a weak spot in the tight fence. He rooted up several of my plants! The fence had kept him out for three years! When he ruined the bed four years earlier, I had painted a large flagstone with these words: "Armadillo was here." I put decorative bark in the bed and displayed the painted stone in the middle as my excuse for no flowers. Lol. Then three years ago Bill installed little fences for me, and I have had seasonal annuals in there again, ever since. It seems like I am always changing out something in that bed. Earlier this week I finally removed the armadillo monument. Lol. He got me! I did not realize that when I fell over the fence it had become unattached to the little poles that kept it snug. It was actually unattached on two poles. We had to work on the bed but laughed that the silly armadillo was so persistent. Like I said, he had not gotten in that bed in three years. That is a pretty good record for me. He had nosed all around on numerous occasions. We had trapped and relocated two armadillos during this time. They just love my flower beds. That was a painful laugh, but still a laugh.

What else can we laugh about today? Oh, yeah! Bill has built a storage building using only wood that he has milled on the sawmill. A pretty amazing project it is! This morning he began to build the wooden door that he will hang. Somehow he lost a washer about one inch in diameter. He looked and looked before he called in the big guns – me, of course.

"I had the washer right here on this table! The nut is still laying right there. But the washer is gone." I looked the table over again. He repeated, "I just had it. I didn't go anywhere. Yet it is gone!" I looked around the nut. I picked up his drill.

It was not under there. The table was a small fold up card table. Bill walked off. "So frustrating! I just had it in my hand!" He sat down in a chair on the porch as I continued looking. I scanned the ground all around the table.

"Is your drill magnetic?" I asked. "It could have slung it off or moved it."

"No! I just had the washer!"

I looked again at the table. I mean, I hated to move anything. After all, this was Bill's stuff, and I surely did not want to mess up his system. There was a set of drill bits that were in a case beside the drill. The case had lots of drill bits. They were organized in slots, and you could turn the slots, sort of like pages in a book. Each "page" had five or six drill bits organized by size and length. I am thinking, "Do not touch his stuff! He may have it open to this "page" for a reason. If you move anything one could fall out or you might lose his place. Do not touch it!" But before I could even get another thought, I reached out and turned the "page" of drill bits. There was the washer!

Surprised, I hollered out, "Bill! Here it is!"

"What? Where was it?"

"I just turned the "page" and there it was!"

"What page? What are you talking about?"

I answered, "I just turned the "page" in the drill bit case and there it was!"

By this time Bill was at the table and he could see the washer, lying there on top of the drill bits. I moved the encased bits and said, "See, I turned the page!"

He shook his head. "So, you turned the 'page,' huh?" He laughed. "Thank you very much!"

"Any time!" I had moved the drill bit slots and nothing had fallen out! The washer was found! The project was saved! Lol.

I hope you laughed a bit. Well, I hope you laughed a lot. Proverbs 17:22 (KJV) declares "A merry heart doeth good like a medicine: but a broken spirit drieth the bones." We don't need any dry bones. Laugh! At least, smile! I recall Evangelist Don Normand, who used to say, "A merry heart doeth good like a 'med-sen'." He was from South Africa and said that Americans pronounce medicine incorrectly. He declared that it is a two-syllable word. "Definitely not 'med-i-cine' as you Americans say. It is 'med-sen.' "

Wishing you a merry heart.

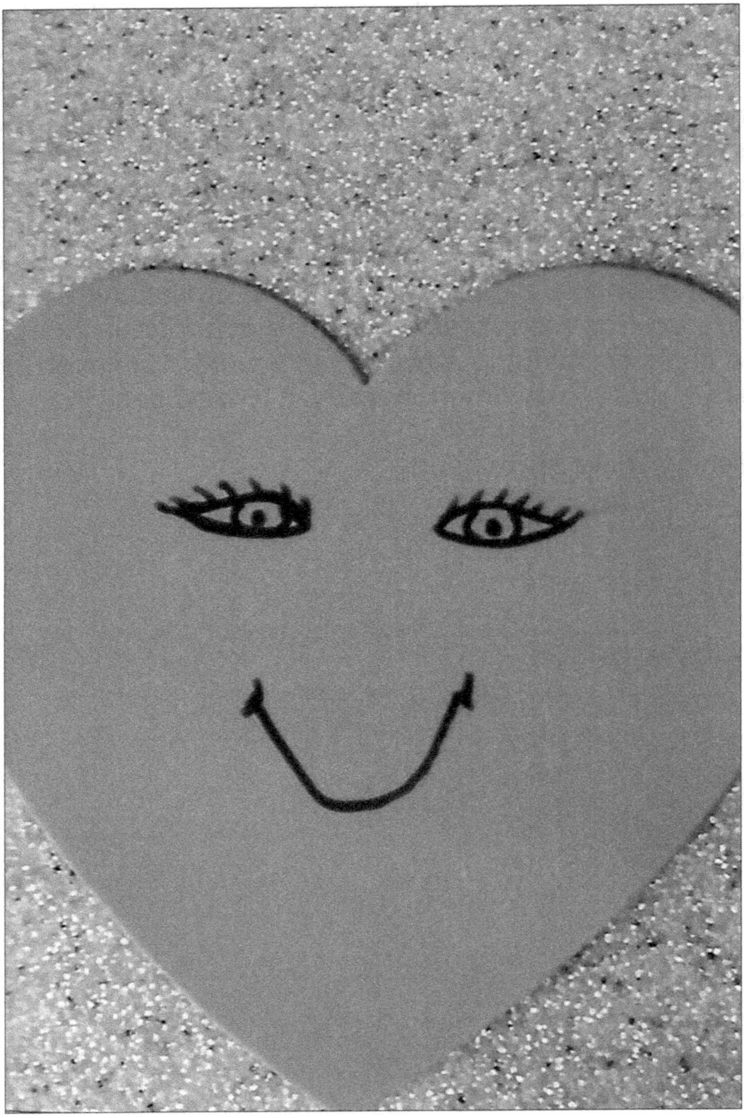

Give Time to God

The secret to having more time?
It makes no sense; it has no rhyme!
"It is to give your time away;
To give your time away, I say!"

Don't know how it works, but it does.
When life was crammed the answer was
"Give time to God, He prospers it."
Time and time again I've seen it.

College classes, mother of three
Clean the house; shop for grocery;
Many clothes to wash, food to cook,
Study all that required homework.

Praise Team practice, six on Tuesday
"I am pianist, so okay –
Absolutely no time to go,
But will be there. I won't say no."

"I'm nuts! I need to wash the clothes!
I pledge to give my time; God knows.
I will head to practice first.
My other chores? I hope no worse!"

How did it work? It filled my cup!
Although I thought I gave it up,
The sacrifice of time I made
It circled back to me some way.

The kids jumped in to help fold clothes.
They smiled as dishwasher door closed.
My new recipes cooked so fast;
Less shoppers in line as I dashed.

Even street lights seemed to smile.
Saw more greens there's no denial.
My heart gave thanks as I drove through,
"God, I love time managed by YOU!"

Give Time to God

Dear Reader,

I hope that your spirit has been lifted and that your walk with God has been enriched by reading this book. I hope you simply enjoyed the ride. I am available for book signings and am willing to speak at your Library, your Book club, your school, or your church group.

We need good literature in the world, and I am doing my part by being faithful to write the things that God has impressed me to write. Thank you for reading my book.

Blessings,

Alice Hein Schiel

abschiel@gmail.com is my email address

CPSIA information can be obtained
at www.ICGtesting.com
Printed in the USA
BVHW012340311022
650745BV00003B/11

9 781662 862625